WISDOM TO SHARE
From Birth to College

Nancy Devlin, Ph.D.

authorHOUSE®

AuthorHouse™
1663 Liberty Drive
Bloomington, IN 47403
www.authorhouse.com
Phone: 1 (800) 839-8640

Published by AuthorHouse 12/26/2017

ISBN: 978-1-5462-1721-3 (sc)
ISBN: 978-1-5462-1720-6 (e)

This book is dedicated to all parents. I regard as parents all you caring people who have accepted the awesome commitment to raise a child to responsible adulthood. You deserve to be loved, cherished and encouraged.

You are the bows from which your children as living arrows are sent forth. The Archer sees the mark upon the path of the Infinite, and He bends you with His might that His arrows may go swift and far. Let your bending in the Archer's hand be for gladness. For even as He loves the arrow that flies, so He loves the bow that is stable.

THE PROPHET
Kahlil Gibran

For clarity I have consistently used female pronouns when referring to teachers and male pronouns when referring to students. Our language, at present, offers only cumbersome alternatives to gender-biased pronouns.

Contents

Cassandra's Classroom: Innovative Solutions for Education Reform 99

Read To Me Talk To Me Listen To Me

Your Child's First Three Years

1

Introduction

We know the country has a problem when a woman says: "I don't work." "I'm just a stay-at-home mother." Or even, "I'm just a housewife." These words are said humbly and apologetically in answer to the question, "What do you do?"

"Just a mother" is the highest calling one can have. The problem is that no one believes this: not the mother, not the workplace and not the government.

We know the mother does not believe it because even before the baby is born, plans have been made for somebody else to take care of him. This, in spite of the fact that all of the studies unequivocally find that what is best for the baby is for his mother to nurture and if possible to breast feed him for at least the first six months.

We know that the workplace does not believe this because a law had to be passed before employers would give mothers the right to stay home in order to nurture their new babies. The "Family and Medical Leave Act" allows mothers to take up to twelve unpaid weeks off, without risking their jobs, to care for the newborn baby. Many employers do not inform their employees of their rights under this law nor do they post the notice as required by law.

Even when informed, many women do not take advantage of the law because they fear it will affect their careers and future earnings if they take off six months, let alone three years to raise their child. This, in spite of the fact that women live longer and will be in the work force longer.

Three years seems a short time to take out of a career that can span over thirty or forty years.

We know that the government does not believe this because it is willing to subsidize day care but not mother care. In the case of the welfare mother, it is making it impossible for her to stay home with her new baby. The government, in compiling its statistics, does not acknowledge the productive work of the mother and her contribution to the economy since what she contributes is unremunerated. Only paid work is recognized and recorded. In case the men who originate these rules and develop these statistics have not noticed, motherhood IS work.

Day care, no matter how well done, is no substitute for the parent. The mother is critical for the first six months and essential for the first three years.

A mother knows her baby best. The baby thrives with the mother who smothers him with love and who is always there for him. A baby needs one-to-one attention and has difficulty relating to the many, often unfamiliar, adults he encounters in day care. In order to thrive, babies need permanence, continuity, passion and commitment. A mother has these qualities in abundance. Let us all strive to help her to do her job and to be what the world needs most --"just a mother."

2

Politicians

Many candidates for president do not seem to have a good education agenda. This could be because they know too little about the topic to have any agenda. The following is an attempt to educate them for the future.

Of all creatures, humans at birth are the least equipped with innate mechanisms needed for survival. Their brains are not fully developed. This makes them amazingly adaptable but exceedingly vulnerable requiring a huge investment by the adults who care for them.

It also forces each baby to go through the process of development, which can only be done by acting on and reacting to the environment. Babies, when stimulated, rapidly learn to influence their environment, to adapt it to themselves and to learn about it by exploring it. Every baby needs to experience this in order for the brain to develop and for learning to take place.

The basic building blocks for the baby's future development are laid from birth to age three because of the plasticity of the brain at these ages. If the brain is not stimulated during that time, as one researcher put it, the "windows of opportunity" are permanently closed. Age three or five, when children go to school, is too late. Children who have not been stimulated are already at a disadvantage and may never catch up.

Babies who began life ready to explore and to live the great adventure are easily defeated by adults who discourage their inquisitiveness and who do not express joy in each new achievement. These babies eventually give up and become lackadaisical. Some babies are left in playpens with bottles in their mouths and the television on for long periods of time by caretakers who are overwhelmed.

Politicians, instead of making educational policies about getting tough with students and the educational establishment, (which is like closing the barn door after the horses have escaped) should be making policies about prevention. The damage has been done before the child comes to school.

Get-tough pronouncements that demand that welfare mothers go to work forces them to depend on day care. These women are taken out of their homes and away from their children with little to show for it because of the high cost of this day care. Instead of these get-tough policies, politicians would be doing the babies a favor by setting up a program to educate the mothers so that they have the opportunity to provide the stimulating environment the babies so desperately need.

Instead of punishing welfare mothers by forcing them out of the home, a system should be developed whereby welfare mothers could stay home and still get their benefits. All politicians need to understand child development if they are going to make decisions that affect the welfare of the family. They need to understand that many children are not succeeding in school because their "windows of opportunity" for intellectual, physical, social and emotional growth were closed long before they arrived at the school door.

Politicians of good faith, please remember the children. They are our only hope for the future.

3

Motherhood as a Profession

Being an at-home mother especially during a baby's first three years of life has to be raised to the status of a profession like doctor, lawyer and teacher. As in any profession, in order to be licensed to practice, one has to finish a course of study and to complete an internship. After successfully completing training and entering the child-rearing profession, a mother, like every other professional, would receive a salary commensurate with her training and experience.

Sound far fetched? Maybe not. Maybe something as dramatic as giving motherhood the best the country has to give in terms of money, education, support and prestige is the only thing that is going to save our neglected children and ensure a brighter future for our country. In our status-conscious society, motherhood is about as low as you can get. At the top are athletes, movie stars, and other celebrities, who contribute little if anything to the country's well-being.

The reason motherhood should be given the high status of a profession is that every profession polices its members because all suffer when one performs badly. We suffer too. Deficient doctors endanger our lives. Deficient lawyers exaggerate our quarrels. Deficient teachers perpetuate our ignorance. And, as was pointed out by James Q. Wilson of UCLA, deficient parents produce poor citizens.

We cannot afford to continue to neglect our nation's babies. It is no longer a question of maybe or maybe not or when we get around to it. It is a question of our survival, not in the future, but NOW.

Mothers and teachers are in lonely professions. They are expected to spend most of their day with children, usually with little or no relief. Guiding children to become responsible adults is a noble calling and used to be very satisfying because mothers and teachers were respected for a job well-done. Our culture, however, no longer holds women who take on these roles in such esteem and their task has become difficult and isolated. Many women who would be excellent mothers and teachers are choosing other professions

Society expects today's mothers to do the job alone. There is no support system for them. Mothers used to have grandparents and other relatives nearby whom they could count on to help. Grandmother lived within walking distance and the children could go on their own to visit her. Now grandparents may live half a continent away and probably have full time jobs. Often mothers lack even a friendly neighbor to visit for adult companionship or to share stories about each others children. The neighbors all go to work.

A mother once apologized to me because she was not working. (It is interesting that she did not equate staying at home to raise her children as work.) She felt inadequate and out of place in our modern society. I asked her how many children had her name down as the person the school should call in an emergency. She quickly added up in her head the names of sixteen children. Obviously she would have upset the equilibrium of the whole neighborhood if she had gone to work. A number of "working" mothers were counting on her. Unfortunately, so few women stay at home that the ones who do have no one to share the burden and this adds to the difficulty of their situation.

Parents of nursery school age children face a similar dilemma. Whether they want to or not they send their children to nursery school at a young age because there are no children left in the neighborhood for them to play with.

Teachers have some of the same needs as mothers who spend a great part of their day with children. Their work can be draining and exhausting. They need intellectual stimulation and meaningful contact with other adults, and like mothers, approval for what they are doing. They also should be provided with the opportunity of sharing their ideas and feelings with other adults. Teachers and today's "non-working" mothers are regarded as low in the "pecking order" in today's culture.

The recent focus on education and teachers may result in some relief for the teachers. There has not been similar focus on the problems of the lonely mothers. Until there is, more and more women will be persuaded to turn their energies and skills outward, away from their children, or to avoid motherhood entirely. I fear this bodes ill for the future of our children and our country.

4

Career and Children

It is time that we as a nation stop squandering our most precious resource--our children.

It is not enough for parents to bring children into the world and only provide food, clothing and shelter for them. Children also need to be nurtured, socialized and educated. If parents, for whatever reason, cannot fulfill this responsibility, then somebody else has to take over. Otherwise, the next generation will suffer.

The first thing that can be done is to make it easy, acceptable and pleasant for mothers to stay home with their children if they so desire especially for the first three years of the child's life. Career versus children does not have to be an either-or proposition. Women should not be put at a professional disadvantage in their careers in order to raise their children. The two are not incompatible. As a matter of fact, it is important that successful career women be given the opportunity to raise their children because they probably have much to offer them. One of the skills the baby acquires during this time is the ability to communicate and to use language. This skill is developed by close interaction with the adults in the environment. Language does not seem to be taught, but rather, it is caught by the baby being stimulated to communicate. Unless such stimulation occurs, receptive and expressive language acquisition may be impaired.

Parents who work are forced to depend on others to provide the necessary stimulation, encouragement, and nurturing needed for the baby's proper development. If this substitute care is not adequate, the baby's development may suffer. When this happens to enough babies, the nation suffers.

Probably one of the least paid are the people hired to take charge of young babies. It is almost impossible for the parents to supervise what is happening to their babies because they are at work. If this is their only or first child, they lack guidelines to know if their child is developing satisfactorily, or if they should be concerned because something is not right with the child. Sometimes the parents do not have enough experience to know what their child needs in the way of care in order for normal development to take place so they cannot judge the quality of the care the child is receiving.

One mother of an infant expressed concern when she realized that her baby was in a room with several other babies with the gate closed and the television turned on. They were not stimulated but were encouraged to sleep. Children in such environments are likely to fall behind others in more stimulating situations who have the warm, lively companionship of caring adults overseeing the children's exploration of their universe.

It is time the nation begins to realize that it needs to be concerned about supervision of childcare personnel. It is time to force employers to give time off to parents who want to raise their children without jeopardizing their job security. It is especially time for the nation to raise the role of parenting to the high level it deserves.

5

Development

Believe in yourself. You are the expert as far as your child is concerned. You know your child better than anyone and, based on this knowledge, you are well equipped to decide what is best for him. In order to do this, however, you need information about child development.

Babies come from the womb not fully developed. They make the greatest spurts in development in the first three years of their lives. During these spurts, they go full-speed-ahead unless someone or something stops them. And we let them, and rejoice in their every accomplishment.

There is no need to accelerate or delay an infant's rate of development. We cannot make a baby walk until he is ready to do so anyhow. A baby learns by actively exploring his environment. Keeping him in a crib or playpen in front of television prevents him from doing this. Babies whose urge to explore is thwarted fail to thrive, become passive, and never really develop a zest for learning. They rarely make up for the time lost in those first three years. I mention this in case your baby is in day care. Many day care services are well aware of these facts, and they are careful to encourage an infant's exploration. It is important for you to know if your child's day care center allows and encourages his explorations. We allow very young children to play and to develop in their own unique way usually until age three. Then we tend to intervene because "play time is over."

Some people are impatient for their child to learn at a very early age. After their child reaches three years, "learning", for many parents, means the things taught in school. They characterize anything else as play and regard it as waste of valuable time. Recent studies have shown that play is an important part of a child's development. In studies of animals, it was found that play stimulates circuits in the brain and helps to tame hostile impulses. The researchers believe the same is true for children. Play is so important to the growing child that parents should initiate it with their babies and encourage it thereafter. As the saying goes: "Play is the work of childhood."

Research also indicates that children who play alone or with others often become more creative and imaginative. Those who can be preoccupied for a long time with toys seem to be able to concentrate for longer periods of time as adults. Also, children who play regularly with peers seem to be better-adjusted adults and have developed good socialization skills.

Take very seriously a related saying: "All work and no play makes Jack a dull boy." School-type activities are usually imposed by adults, while play is usually created by the child, providing opportunity for self-discovery, creativity and use of the imagination. Some parents on hearing this might decide to introduce "mandatory play" as a way to foster their child's development. When adults attempt to control and to direct play, it is no longer play, and is rarely fun or helpful to the developing child.

We might try to bring back the spirit of play to all our endeavors. I encourage you to do it not only for your children, but for yourself. It would certainly make all of our lives more pleasant and less stressful.

6

First Three Years

Unlike most of the animals of the wild, born physically capable of taking care of their needs, the human child emerges from the womb unfinished. Much of his development takes place after birth in the extraordinary first three years of life. How the body and brain grows and develops during this period will affect the human child forever.

Our society is presently engaged in a furious controversy about protecting the child in the womb, but it is criminally negligent concerning the vital years following birth. What is so extraordinary about this knowledge is that its implications for future generations is ignored. Some of today's parents have children without intending to personally follow through with their children's development during this crucial time. They leave that to others.

That leaves the educational system with children who probably will never reach their full potential. By school age, scientists tell us, the plasticity of the brain is gone. We keep trying to make up for those years by many different kinds of school reforms. We bewail the fact that students do not seem to be as well prepared as they once were. We blame it on the curriculum and lack of behavioral and intellectual discipline, and we try to make appropriate adjustments. Nothing seems to change. Parents blame schools and teachers and demand that they do something for the students. What a pity. Nobody seems willing to protect and to nurture the very young child so that he has a brighter future.

Ultimately parents are responsible. Recent studies carried out over many years in six regions of North America found a consistent correlation between quality of family life and level of cognitive development during the first three years of life. Parental attentiveness and availability of stimulating play proved more strongly related to child development status than global measures of environmental quality such as socioeconomic status.

Enough is known about early child development to help parents become effective teachers of their developing children. One program, "Parents as First Teachers", was developed for the Missouri school system by Dr. Burton White, of the Center for Parent Education in Massachusetts. Parents enrolled in this program were helped from the third trimester of their pregnancy to their child's third birthday. The evaluation of this program indicated that these children scored significantly higher on all measures of intelligence, achievement, auditory comprehension, verbal ability and language ability than did comparison children. They also demonstrated more positive social development, including ability to work well with adults. These parents also were more likely than a comparison group to rate their school districts as responsive to their children's needs.

Several recommendations should be obvious from these data. Effective parenting skills can be learned. The best time to learn them is before becoming a parent. A course like "Parents as First Teachers" should be required of every high school student, both male and female. It could be one of the most important courses given in our schools. It should be a highly regarded course and it should be staffed with outstanding teachers.

The other recommendation is that businesses encourage their women employees, who choose to have children, to stay home with them for the first three years. These women should be assured that their job will be waiting for them when they return. It would be even better, if these mothers were subsidized so that staying home would not be a financial burden to the family. It seems strange that big businesses oppose this idea while at the same time they deplore the intellectual and educational deficiencies of their workers. They are forced to spend a great deal of money on remedial education. Why not spend some of that money on prevention? We are becoming a nation of people who do not care what happens to the next generation.

1

Play

Parents of preschool children are concerned about learning and want to provide the best for their children so that they will be ready for "real" school. In an effort to do everything right, parents turn to the experts and attempt to follow them even though the experts may disagree on what should be done. As a result, the parents are confused.

More and more parents are following advice on what they believe will help the intellectual development of the child, while the other aspects of the child's development are being relegated to a less important role. I believe this is done because intellectual development can be charted, evaluated, observed and taught. Also, parents have many commercial tools at their disposal to help them as they interact with the children in this realm. They can buy books for the children and read to them. They can buy crayons and coloring books and teach them the colors. They can buy scissors and paper to help them with cutting. The list of things to buy is almost endless - games, puzzles, computers. As a result, some children come to school with these skills while others may have been neglected. The problem becomes compounded by the fact that many schools now conduct the kindergarten program as a downward extension of the regular school program so that other important developmental areas are ignored.

Besides intellectual development, we must be concerned with the physical, emotional and social development of the child. These areas seem vague and not as concrete as the intellectual area. They are difficult to evaluate quantitatively, but they are just as important. In addition, there is the danger that if we concentrate on the academic skill aspect of the child's development to the exclusion of the rest, we may be asking children to do tasks that are inappropriate for their level of total development.

Children who by five years old should have had a great deal of experience being physically active. They should have had opportunities to hop, to jump and later, to skip. They should have been helped to develop independence and be now able to wash, to dress and to feed themselves and to use the toilet. They should have had opportunities to play with their peers in dramatic play where they can take on a variety of roles. They should have the beginnings of social skills.

Children need many opportunities to interact with the objects, materials and people in their environment. These activities include block building, measuring, weighing, planting, pouring, filling, playing in the sand box and so on. They are concrete thinkers and need to interact with concrete objects, not just books and pencil and paper. Children should be encouraged to be active and not passive learners.

Children benefit when given opportunities for spontaneous play. This helps them to learn about themselves and others, to learn how to get along with others, and to learn about reality. Children at this age need to be given many opportunities to explore their world. They are not empty vessels to be filled by teachers with facts. They need actual, real-life experiences first before they can deal with abstract concepts. When a child predicts that something will happen, the adult's response should be: "Let's find out." The process of finding out is more important at this level than the correct answer.

Young children need a rich physical environment and space in which to explore this environment. They also need time to integrate and practice new skills. This is best accomplished in an atmosphere that is child-centered and not adult task-oriented. There should be movement, activity, singing, dancing, nurturing, exploring and finding out. Parents can best help their children by providing such an atmosphere at home and by monitoring the programs provided for their children in school settings.

8

Independence

There is a saying in the world of real estate that to successfully buy a house you should consider three things: location, location, location. In the world of parenting to successfully raise children you must do three things: anticipate, anticipate, anticipate. Parents who have learned to do this make their lives easier. Here are just a few examples.

The first thing to anticipate is that your baby is going to become mobile one day. Anticipate that day by childproofing your home. Get down on your hands and knees and see the world from your child's viewpoint. Cover all electrical outlets. Put locks on all closets that have cleaning material in them. Put away or out-of-reach all of your breakable possessions. Notice which pieces of furniture have sharp edges and either cover them or remove them. Anticipation in this instance allows your child to explore his world safely and happily. It is much better than thwarting your child's development by constantly saying "No" to protect him.

The next thing to anticipate is that as your baby grows, he is going to start to develop his own personality and to strive to become independent. In order to do this, he is going to start to say "No" no matter what the request is. You have not failed as a parent. The child needs to do this to grow. The best thing to do is not to make too many verbal requests. When you really want him to do something, pick him up and put him where you want him to be. This works better than a lot of talking and explaining. Too much discussion usually falls on deaf ears. Some parents get upset because they are afraid their child lacks discipline and is thwarting their authority.

They then resort to physical punishment. If you anticipate this stage, you will not be threatened and will discipline appropriately.

In the same vein, it helps to anticipate which activities are going to cause difficulty for your child. If he has a short attention span, do not insist that he go shopping with you for two to three hours when you know from past experience that he gets upset and negative. Spanking a child because he gets cranky is not useful especially when you could have predicted the behavior. Anticipating that he will get cranky allows you to take appropriate steps ahead of time.

This applies to other situations where children might have difficulty. Two such situations are visiting relatives, and eating in restaurants. Some relatives have a difficult time with children. They do not take precautions by putting away their favorite vase and get very upset when something gets broken. Anticipate this by asking them to be aware that children like to explore. Or, you could limit the amount of time you stay with those relatives. Most children can control their behavior for just so long. Asking them not to touch anything for four or five hours may be asking too much.

This is also true for taking children out to restaurants. Try it and see how they behave. If they cannot handle it, it is best to take them home immediately and to try again at a later time. Embarrassing you and them in the restaurant is not productive and shows lack of anticipation. You could practice proper behavior at home before trying again.

In order to anticipate behavior, it helps to know about children's developmental stages. Your librarian can recommend many suitable books. It also helps to know your unique child well. When you get good at anticipation, you will find yourself using the "No" word less and less with your children. As a result, their lives and yours will be much more pleasant.

9

Too Soon

In an effort to give the best to our children we sometimes do too much too soon. We are then surprised when things do not turn out as well as we expected. Instead of rushing and planning ahead for our children, we might be more helpful if we took time to find out who they are and gave them time to develop their own unique personalities.

There are a growing number of educational programs for young children that introduce preschoolers to symbolic rules and rote learning too soon. Instead of workbook drills and spelling exercises, the children should be exposed to learning experiences that are self-directed and take into account the children's natural curiosity and motivation. Children who have spent many years in day care programs are not more ready for academic instruction at an earlier age than children who have not had this experience.

Research indicates that readiness and maturity are more critical for success in kindergarten than previous preschool or day care experience. Research also indicates that children who are taught to read at a very early age are no further ahead of their classmates by grade three than those children who were taught later when they were developmentally ready to acquire the skills and knowledge offered.

Adults tend to want to get on with it and speed up the process of learning. Some parents are under the mistaken impression that a child's intelligence is based on how well he can read and use language. Therefore, the reasoning goes, the sooner he learns to read, the more intelligent he will be. This is a very shortsighted definition of intelligence and learning.

A child needs to develop many other types of intelligence: linguistic, musical, logical-mathematical, spatial, bodily-kinesthetic and personal. Many children fail to develop in these other areas because adults tend to value only the verbal-academic.

Well-meaning parents need to resist the tendency to give in to advertising which tells them: How to Raise a Brighter Child, Kindergarten is Too Late, How to Teach Your Baby to Read, How to Give Your Baby Encyclopedic Knowledge. More is not better. What is better is to match our teaching to what the children are developmentally ready to learn. Otherwise, we may produce children with poor self-concepts and low motivation to learn. We cannot teach a six-month-old baby to walk if he is not developmentally ready to do so, nor can we teach him to run before he walks.

Parents can best help their children by acknowledging that all children develop and mature at different rates and the rate of development has nothing to do with intelligence. Parents who attempt to accelerate this rate are doing their children a disservice and causing them to be stressed unnecessarily.

Parents may need to monitor the programs their children are being offered at school to be certain that they take into account the developmental level of the children. This is especially true of kindergarten programs.

Schools could solve this problem by eliminating grade designations and calling schools the primary, the intermediate and the high school units. Some children might take five years to complete the primary unit while others might take six or seven. Children who develop on a slower or faster timetable should not be penalized. The goal of schooling should be to help all children reach their fullest potential.

The verb, "to educate", means "to lead", "to draw out", "to develop". It does not imply changing children into something they are not.

10

Decide to Work

Women who leave work to have a child often have a difficult decision to make after the birth of the child. They must decide when to go back to work. It is important that parents have the information necessary for an informed decision. The final decision is theirs and once made, parents should not be made to feel guilty no matter what their decision. Many new parents, however, are uninformed about child development and sometimes make this irrevocable decision based on lack of information.

Dr. Burton White of the Center for Parent Education has worked for over twenty years observing babies from birth to three years of age. His studies indicate that these years are critical for children's ultimate educational development and that the best teachers are the parents and grandparents. These are the people who give the children the incentive to grow and to develop by their deep love and encouragement. They are the baby's first cheering section as each milestone is passed. For the new parents and grandparents, seeing the child learn to take his first step or say his first word produces genuine and delightful fuss in which the baby basks and grows.

Babies need to explore their environment to learn. Their curiosity can decline if they are too restricted. They need someone to watch them so that they can explore safely. They need someone to help them when they get stuck. This takes a commitment on the part of the adult and the people who are most committed are the parents and grandparents.

Dr. White is so convinced of the importance of parents and grandparents in providing care for the first three years of life that he recommends that the government provide support and assistance to the family so that the parents can provide this care rather than providing support for day care centers. He recommends a parent education program for families so that they can provide their children's first educational delivery system. Intervention should begin at the earliest age possible and should improve the child's home environment by sensitizing the parents to the child's developmental needs.

Parents need to know about developmental stages in order to be prepared to help their child develop language and social skills. Part of this preparedness requires that they be alert to physical and sensory handicaps. Dr. White is especially concerned about hearing loss. When it occurs, detecting and responding to the loss is crucial. During the first three years of life, children undergo rapid, basic language learning. Delay in acquiring language skills is one of the most common causes of under-achieving in school. Being able to hear is essential to the development of receptive language in a young baby. Parents need to know about the importance of talking to babies. The baby should begin to understand speech even though she cannot talk herself.

The first three years constitute a once-in-a-lifetime opportunity for the child to attain good language skills in addition to a sense of curiosity about the world around her. Many other essential skills are acquired during this period. It is the time when the child develops a sense of trust and learns that she is loved and safe. The child begins the development of good interpersonal skills. This is not a haphazard process or one that can be left to chance. Dr. White feels it is harder to produce a happy and nice child than it is to produce a smart one. Parents have to make a decision about their children and how they want them to develop. It takes work and commitment but putting the commitment into these first three years will make the rest of the job easier and more successful.

11

Hearing and Language

The first thing to be concerned about is whether your child hears correctly. By three months your child should be startled by a loud clap behind him. By six months he should search for the source of a sound by turning his eyes and head. By ten months he should respond to his own name or to a telephone ringing. By fifteen months he should be able to look at familiar objects when asked to and imitate simple sounds and words. No child is too young for a hearing test. Tests should be given more than once and at different times. If you have concerns or doubts go to a specialist.

Your child should be developing receptive and expressive language skills. Receptive skills refer to how well your child understands language. Expressive skills refer to the production of language. All children understand more than they can or do express. A stimulating environment helps them to develop in both areas. In expressive language development,

- by three months he should be babbling,
- by six months, he should be expressing eagerness and vocalizing pleasure and displeasure,
- by eight months, he should be producing different sounds like "ba", "da", "ka".
- by ten months, he should be able to shout to attract attention and may say "mamma" and "dada",
- by twelve months, he should be able to repeat familiar words by imitation.

Dr. Patricia Kuhl of the University of Washington says that mothers who talk "motherese" with its high pitch, exaggerated intonation and clear pronunciation, help babies acquire phonetic prototypes which are the building blocks of language. Parents should talk to their babies often in order for them to hear the sounds which help to develop language.

We could all use a sitter like John Travolta in the movie, "Look Who's Talking". The character played by Travolta took care of the baby for a year. He did not take the easy way out and put the baby in the crib and pacify him with a bottle. Instead, he talked to him constantly. He took him to see an airplane and talked to the baby all of the time about what he was seeing. As Travolta drove the car, he talked through all the actions that he was taking: "first you put the key in, then you push down on the pedals, then you turn the steering wheel." This baby was being stimulated to learn all of the time he was with Travolta.

Dr. Jean Piaget, the Swiss scholar whose greatest research was on how the child develops, would endorse Travolta's method. In his studies of very young children Piaget found that the more new things the baby sees and hears, the more new things he will be interested in seeing and hearing. The idea is to keep the baby interested as he develops. This is the period when the child develops a zest for wonder.

12

Testing and Teaching

The teaching of reading and writing in kindergarten until recently was not permitted. Now we have tests to determine if children are ready for the kindergarten curriculum that includes reading and writing.

Many school systems test children before they come to kindergarten. As a result of these tests some children are declared more ready than others. This can have a devastating affect on the parents. For five years the parents have been very happy watching and helping their child develop. Then the child is given a test, usually lasting less than a half hour, and the parents are led to believe that in some way their child is deficient. He or she is not ready for kindergarten. Parents not only can lose confidence in themselves they can lose confidence in their child. Their wonderful child is somehow wanting in the eyes of the world. It does not matter that the child is performing well within the range of normal development, that the tests have big uncertainties, and that rates of development vary considerably. All the parent takes away from the testing is the feeling that there is something wrong.

One of the goals of the school should be to inspire a parent to have confidence in his or her child. This deep-down parental confidence will carry that child a long way. Schools should be finding ways of demonstrating to parents that their children have a chance to succeed in coping with life, rather than giving a negative message which deprives them of confidence in themselves and their children. Nothing is more disheartening than an expectation of hopelessness and failure for one's own child.

Dr. Harriet Egertson, of the National Association of Early Childhood Specialists, makes a plea for recapturing kindergarten for five-year olds. Twenty years earlier, she reminds us, no one worried whether children had long attention spans, whether they could count to 20, say their ABC's or know their sounds because it was expected that school would teach these things in good time. There was no imposed kindergarten readiness criteria based on eye-hand coordination or auditory and visual memory because the materials and equipment were designed to help these capacities to emerge.

Today the kindergarten curriculum is at least one year accelerated, requiring the teaching of specific skills that the children are expected to learn. Dr. Egertson goes on to bemoan the fact that rich, creative experiences with real materials like blocks, clay, paint and dramatic play props have been replaced by worksheets, workbooks, and other didactic tasks. She believes that children spend too much time practicing, over and over, a narrow spectrum of discrete skills that are seldom tied to anything young children care about, are interested in, or need. Also many of these tasks are just plain boring which deadens the enthusiasm for learning that children bring with them. Worse, they cause many children to feel like failures.

There used to be a separate certification for teaching kindergarten. Now teachers have one certification for kindergarten to eighth grade. An eighth grade teacher can be reassigned to teach kindergarten with no extra special training.

13

Empathy

Being able to put oneself in another's place, to feel what he feels and to understand what he understands is an attribute necessary for the survival of the human race. Its development is so important that it cannot be left to chance. It has to be consciously modeled and taught. Empathetic adults produce empathetic children.

Parents can help their child to develop this trait by first providing opportunities for him to understand and to practice using words that express feelings. Words like angry, happy, sad can be displayed on the refrigerator door with the appropriate pictures beside them. The child can help pick out pictures that express emotion from magazines or he can draw them himself.

Once the concrete-thinking child understands what the words mean, parents can begin to use them in order to help the child to understand how his actions affect others. "When you hit your brother, he gets upset and cries because it hurts." "Taking your friend's toy without asking makes him feel sad." "I feel happy because you helped me by picking up your toys."

These concepts can be reinforced through stories in books and on television. As you read the story, ask your child how he thinks the character in the story feels and why. If he says the character is sad, ask your child what he would do to make him happy. If one of the characters is mean, ask what he could do to help the mean child not feel so bad. Ask how he would feel if somebody did that to him. Use the breaks provided by commercials to ask the same questions regarding the TV program you are watching. Using TV this way makes it an active and not a passive activity.

If possible, it helps to have a family pet like a cat or dog that the child can relate to and perhaps be responsible for. A pet responds to kindness with affection. A mistreated animal, on the other hand, responds by becoming withdrawn or by being aggressive. These responses give children concrete, almost instantaneous feedback, that all actions, both positive and negative have consequences.

Cruelty to animals, especially in young children, needs to be given attention. They either do not understand that the animal is suffering or they do understand and they do not care. These are the children who may have never been given the opportunity to experience empathy in their own lives.

On the other hand, it tells you a great deal about a person when he is kind to an animal. Movies use this fact to develop a character's personality quickly. If they want the macho man to have a tender side, they show him taking care of his cat.

Schools can help children by providing opportunities for them not only to experience empathy, but to practice it. This can be done through cooperative learning lessons, school counsels, older children reading to younger ones, food and clothing drives, visiting nursing homes, and so on.

Parents can tell their own stories about how somebody helped them that day or how they helped or understood somebody else. Children should be noticed and encouraged every time they give the empathetic response rather than the negative, mean one. They should be encouraged to tell how it makes them feel when they respond positively to another.

It is never too early to begin to develop empathy in children. Professor Alan Leslie of Rutgers University, in studying the development of perception in infants and young children, found that what can be observed developing in infants becomes a recognizable trait by three to four years of age. By even that young age, a child can infer what another child perceives even though that perception is different from his own.

14

Self-esteem

There is no guaranteed, successful method to ensure that your child will develop positive self-esteem since it is not something you give to a child. He either develops it or he does not. You can, however, promote an atmosphere where it can be nurtured. Children are concrete thinkers and are very observant. Adults are their models. If you model positive self-esteem, it can become catching. Parents who are fearful about making mistakes have a difficult time finding joy and relaxing around their children. The more joy, fun and laughter you can bring into the home, the more your chances are of having happy children who feel good about themselves.

Try to slow down especially when dealing with very young children. Relax with your babies. Babies need to be able to explore their environments safely on their own terms. They need to be encouraged in these explorations and not thwarted. This is the time when babies learn about themselves, their world and become creative explorers. Babies who do not have these opportunities become passive. Parents need only to relax and to be available to take the cues from the baby. You do not need to accelerate this development. Give him time and rejoice in every milestone and he will get there on his own time frame.

Try not to compare his rate of development to others in the family or to the baby down the street. Each child is unique. As the saying goes: Childhood is a Journey not a Race. This is the time in your child's development when you can really relax and enjoy yourself because babies know what they need to do in order to prosper. It only becomes a problem when the parents' agenda interferes with the baby's agenda. We sometimes are in too much of a hurry to get on with it. Not only with the babies' development but with getting and keeping the house perfect or trying to raise perfect children like the children down the street.

We become involved in doing things for the children but not enjoying or taking the time to be with them as persons. Have confidence in yourself and relax and instead of painting the kitchen, sit beside the sandbox, give your child your undivided attention and encourage him to explore. If the lady down the street has children but spends most of her time keeping her house perfect, stop visiting her. Find somebody who is also sitting beside the sandbox letting her child know she enjoys giving him, her undivided attention.

Improve your own self-esteem so that you are a good role model. I hate to tell you but you still cannot get away with: Do as I say, not as I do. When you hear about self-esteem, it always seems to be a case of; "If only the rest of the world would do better by me, I would be okay." It always seems to be dependent on someone else's behavior not your own. You cannot control what the rest of the world will do or not do so you must take responsibility for how you feel about yourself. Once you learn to do this, you can help your children. One way to do this is to distinguish between rational and irrational beliefs.

Irrational:

- Everybody must love me.
- I must be good at everything.
- Some people are bad and must be punished.
- Things should be different.
- It's your fault I feel this way.
- I know something bad will happen soon.
- It's easier not to even try.
- I can't help being this way.
- I need someone stronger than I am.
- I need to get upset about your problems.
- There's only one good way to do it.

Rational:

- Everybody does not have to love me.
- It is okay to make mistakes.
- I do not have to control things
- I am responsible for my day
- I can handle it when things go wrong.
- It is important to try.
- I am capable.
- I can change.
- Other people are capable.
- I can be flexible.

The same parents who are very effective in the workplace and feel good about themselves may not feel good about themselves as parents.

You are the expert as far as your own children are concerned. Trust your judgment. Mistakes may be made, but if we learn from them, they are not failures. The problem for parents today is that there are too many uncontrollable negative outside influences that impact the family. Just to name a few: television, insecure job opportunities, job stress, overworked and overtired parents, world catastrophes, no pleasant or upbeat news in the papers or television, guns in the hands of young people who do not hesitate to use them, and youth gangs. You can add to the list

In order to survive in the world today, all members of the family need to help one another to develop and to nurture self-esteem. The family is the place where all members should be accepted completely as they are, not as they might be, could be, should be--but as they are. This acceptance allows them to go back into the world renewed and able to face most challenges.

15

Praise and Encouragement

All members of the family need to practice encouraging behavior. This includes father to mother, mother to father as well as among the children. When people are only told how incompetent they are, they cease to learn and refuse to take risks. All members of the family need to be told and to be encouraged when they do things right, not just caught and told when they do things wrong.

Start with yourself. Compliment yourself instead of finding fault. "I look good today. That color looks nice on me." Do the same with your family at breakfast. "Mary, I like the way you did your hair. You look nice." "Joe, thanks for getting me the paper. I appreciate your noticing I wanted it." Model accepting compliments. If your husband compliments you on how you are dressed, thank him and avoid making negative comments like, "how could you like this old thing?" If somebody says you did something well, say, "Yes I think so, too," rather than, "Oh, it was nothing."

These words of encouragement should be given constantly -- ten to fifteen times a day at least. Words of encouragement give the message that in your family everyone is accepted as they are, not for what they could or should be. Treat each child uniquely, not equally.

There is a difference between praise and encouragement. Praise is a label and all labels should be avoided. Praise attaches conditional love to behavior. "I'm proud of you. You came in first." "You are a good girl." To build self-esteem, focus on behavior that is appreciated rather than imply that children have more worth as persons if they excel. Children must feel that their person is cherished, independent of their behavior.

This is called separating the deed from the doer. Examples kinds of labels tend to stick: "Sally is slow developing. Her sister walked much sooner." Other examples of negative are labels are: uncommunicative, shy, slow, unfeeling, and unaffectionate. Describe behavior but do not label. "Sally has a difficult time in new situations. It takes her awhile to warm up, but she does eventually when she feels comfortable. I usually give her more time to get used to new things instead of forcing her to do it right away." Sally may grow out of the behavior, but all of her life she could be stuck with the label of the shy one in the family and find it difficult to change this impression and perhaps develop into a different person.

Learn to use "I" statements and not "You" statements. Never say anything against the child as a person. You can say negative things about the behavior but you accept the child completely as he is, not as he might be, could be, should be--but as he is. He or she is the best thing that ever happened to your family. The "you" statement places blame and labels the child. It is a verbal attack against the person. The "I" statement on the other hand tells how you feel and how the behavior affects you. Describe what you see, what you feel, what you expect. Do not humiliate your child, attack his character or offend his dignity.

"You" statement: "You idiot, look what you did by not watching where you are going. You broke the lamp." "I" statement: "I am upset because the lamp is broken. The next time, put on the light before you look for something in the room." In families, labels tend to stick. If you label the child as a bad person that is what you will get. Remember to treat each child uniquely, not equally. Children are born with different temperaments the same way parents come with different temperaments. Accept and rejoice in these differences and understand them so that your children can develop into the people they were meant to be not into the people you want them to be. Children can develop poor self-esteem when they get the message that their parents wanted a different child from the one they got. A child may get the distinct message that his parents would rather have a gifted soccer player like the kid next door, or a popular cheer leader like the girl down the street, instead of the introverted loner they have who is not like either of his out-going parents. These different temperaments affect how parents respond to each child, how they discipline and how they respond to different child rearing practices.

Provide opportunities for your children to make choices. They need to feel some control over their lives. Along with choice comes accepting the consequences of these choices. Of course, you cannot allow them to come to harm, but otherwise, try not to step in to protect children when their choices do not turn out well. This shows a lack of confidence in them and does not help build self-esteem.

16

Finally

Teach your children to become problem solvers. Competent problem solvers feel good about themselves and children can learn to solve most problems themselves. Resist the temptation to step in and to make the world perfect. The world is not perfect. You know this and have learned that it is okay. You can handle it. Help your children do the same.

Ask yourself the question: Are we as a family enjoying each other and having fun? If the answer is no, rethink what you are doing. Think of ways to bring fun and joy to your life and to your family's life. There has to be someplace where people can be renewed and accepted completely. The best possibility is in the family. Life is too sad otherwise and it does not have to be that way. This might be the time to examine your priorities. I wish you joy as you experience life's greatest adventure -- nurturing and raising children who feel and experience your love.

Arrows Swift & Far: Guiding Your Child Through School

Preface

Never doubt that a small group of thoughtful, committed citizens can change the world. Indeed, it's the only thing that ever has.

Margaret Mead

Your child is going to spend a great part of his life in school. Before he enters school, you are in charge of making all decisions. You can decide whether or not to send him to pre-school programs. You can choose how often to send him, and you can make any changes you feel proper at any time. Suddenly, when your child becomes five, the school system takes over with its many customs, regulations and laws. You now face a system which has been in power for generations. You lose control but still bear primary responsibility for the education of your child.

What can you do? The most important thing you can do is to become informed. That is the goal of this book. To help you to understand the school system so that you can ensure that your child will receive a proper education.

You may never have experienced a good school system yourself. You may not know what the possibilities are, what your rights are or what you can and should expect. You may approach the educational system as the student you once were. Maybe you were reasonably successful at school; maybe not. But in any case, you were taught that the school is the authority, and that you must humbly submit.

Now try to approach the school system as you have learned to approach the health care system. You know how to choose a doctor, a hospital, how to describe symptoms, how to monitor medicines. You keep informed to avoid becoming a victim of the very system that is supposed to be helping you. The same thing should be true of your dealings with the educational system.

You can best help the school system to succeed by being supportive, by encouraging the people in the system and by understanding what schools can and cannot do. It is not enough to complain about what is wrong; you need to know what is right. This means understanding, monitoring, supplementing and, possibly, changing the school system to guarantee that it fulfills its educational mandate.

Our schools have a great deal to offer if you know how to use them well. You are up to the challenge if you have the information needed to deal successfully with the system. When you make decisions about your child, you base them on the information you have at the time. It is important, therefore, for you to acquire the knowledge necessary to make wise and informed decisions. This book is intended to start you on the path to obtaining that knowledge.

1

Kindergarten Screening

"It is the highest creatures who take the longest to mature and are the most helpless during their immaturity."

Bernard Shaw

Did you have to take an entrance exam to get into kindergarten? Were your kindergarten days filled with reading, writing, workbooks and finally the taking of a standardized test? Did you ever fail kindergarten?

Sound ridiculous? Well that is a real possibility for some of today's children. They experience a world different from the one you did, for better or for worse.

Understand the Test Results
Learn How Test Results Are Used
Know When to Give Your Child Another Year

Understand the Test Results

The first contact you will have with the school system will be the kindergarten screening tests. These tests usually include the following:

- Free drawing and figure copying,
- Language comprehension and expression,
- Reasoning and counting,
- Balancing and motor coordination.

It helps to keep in mind that these tests are not infallible. They have big uncertainties and measure neither your child's intelligence nor his ability to do appropriate school work.

Remember that there is great variability in the rate of normal development, but all children get there eventually. As long as your child is following a normal sequence of development, he is okay and you are okay. Do not let anybody tell you anything different.

A very discouraged parent reported the following incident involving her son: She knew that he would be one of the youngest in his kindergarten class and that she probably would not send him but give him another year to develop. However, she felt no harm would be done by his taking the screening test. The results might give her some useful information. That did not happen.

After the testing, she and her husband were summoned to school to a meeting. At this meeting, they were given their son's test results in negative terms. Instead of saying sentences like: "He can do 'this' now because he is four and a half," or "He will learn 'that' later because it is an older skill," the officials described their son by pointing out everything he could not do. These parents were crushed, and, tragically lost some level of confidence in themselves and their son. In addition, their child's test results and interpretations by the school system then became part of his permanent school record.

Schools tend to view children in terms of the rate of the "average" child's development. "Average" is a statistical group concept, and it does not allow for the uniqueness of the development of the individual child. As a result, a child can be declared out of step when, in actual fact, the system is out of step with the child.

You can protect your child's self-esteem if you know the normal sequence of physical, intellectual, emotional and social development of children. If the school begins to tell you what your child cannot do, stop them and have them tell you what he can do. You will be able to judge whether what they say is true for your child if you know, understand, and accept the unique rate at which your child develops early childhood skills.

Early Skills

During the first few years of life, a child learns a staggering array of skills. No subsequent stage of life approaches this period in achievement. Here are just some of the skills acquired:

- gross motor skills: crawling, walking, climbing stairs, running, jumping,
- fine motor skills: grasping and manipulating objects, hand-eye coordination,
- cognitive skills: watching, listening, attention span, color recognition, counting, remembering, time sense, relationships,
- communication skills: understanding and speaking language,
- social skills: recognition of and response to himself and others,
- self-help skills: feeding, dressing and washing himself

Within reasonable limits, the sequence of developmental milestones is more important than the age at which each milestone is passed. The time-tables used in most books are merely approximations and there is great variability, which is normal among children. Be alert, however, for any **serious** delays which could be caused by some physical problem. For example, hearing loss could delay communication skills.

Learn How Test Results Are Used

At one time the teaching of reading and writing in kindergarten was not permitted. Now most schools use kindergarten screening tests to determine if children are ready for the predetermined curriculum which includes these subjects. School systems rarely use these test results to plan a curriculum appropriate for the in-coming kindergarten class. Rather, the test results are used to exclude children the system regards as unready for their first school experience.

As a result, some children are declared more ready than others. This can have a devastating effect on you, as parents. For five years you have been very happy watching and helping your child develop. Then he is given a test, usually lasting less than half an hour, and you are led to believe that in some way your child is deficient. He is not as ready as his peers for kindergarten. You can not only lose confidence in yourself as parents; you can also lose confidence in your child.

Remember in this situation that you are your child's advocate and that you know him best. If the school, after less than half an hour of testing, tells you something about your child that you disagree with, trust your own judgment.

Know When To Give Your Child Another Year

Until school systems change, it might be worthwhile for you to consider giving your young son another year before sending him to kindergarten and enrolling him into the system. I say son because at this age boys develop on a different time-table from girls which makes it harder for them to accomplish the goals set for today's kindergartners. Another year might give him enough time to reach the developmental level necessary to score well on readiness tests and to succeed with today's kindergarten program. So many parents of young boys are doing this now that it may force the school system to re-evaluate its kindergarten curriculum. Currently, many children, especially young boys, are given tasks they are not developmentally ready to do. As a result they lose their enthusiasm for learning and begin to have poor self-images and to think of themselves as failures, unable to learn.

Parents of kindergarten children can best help them by acknowledging that all children develop and mature at different rates and the rate of development has nothing to do with intelligence. Parents who attempt to accelerate this rate are doing their children a disservice and frustrating them unnecessarily. Have confidence in your child and his ability to be successful and he will not disappoint you. At the same time, monitor the kindergarten program to be certain that your child is not being stressed by a program which is too far ahead or too far behind his stage of development.

2

The First Day At School

"There are few successful adults who were not first successful children."

Perspective
Alexander Chase

There is excitement as well as apprehension in the air at the beginning of any school year. This is especially true for children entering school for the first time and for their parents. Similar feelings can be true for older children entering a new school or simply anticipating contact with new classmates. For many, the transition is smooth and free of anxiety. For others, it is a fearful time.

Some Things Children and Parents Fear
How to Prepare For the First Day
The First Day And After

Some Things Children and Parents Fear

By the time your child is ready to enter school for the first time, he is able to anticipate differences between the familiar, comfortable environment at home and this new, strange place called school. Anticipation of the change to school life can be fearful especially if the child does not know what to expect. Sometimes, older children tease younger ones with horror stories about school.

The kindergartner, new to elementary school, may be afraid that his mother will never find him at the end of the day because the school is so big. Or, he may fear that he will get off of the bus at the wrong stop and be lost forever. Or, he might be afraid he will forget his name and address when the teacher asks him and fail his first school task.

There is a Peanuts cartoon in which Sally comes home from her first day at school and says to her brother, Charlie Brown. "You goofed, big brother. You told me to bring a lunch box to school and everybody else brown-bagged it." Charlie Brown's response is: "I can't stand the responsibility." We may all feel that way when even having the wrong lunch box can be viewed as a disaster.

The older child, too, may have anxieties about the first day of a new school year. He may be worried about a new set of classmates or how a new teacher will feel about him. He may fear that they will have no friends or that he will be bullied and cry. He may be unsure that he has the right clothes and fear they will bring him ridicule.

Parents also have fears. They do not know how to protect their children from the hurts they may experience. They fear making wrong decisions because of the conflicting advice they are given on how to help their children. They fear their children will not do well in school and may not be as well prepared as the other students.

How to Prepare For the First Day

The first-day fears of parents and children are real and legitimate. Most resolve themselves in the first few days of school. However, by anticipating them and taking corrective action, the transition can be eased.

For a kindergartner or a child new to a school, it helps if you take him to school before it starts in September. Show your child where you will pick him up. If there is an older sibling in the school, he might go with you to introduce the newcomer to the school. The message to the child is that everyone knows where he is and he will not be forgotten or left alone. If he will be using the bus, show him where it will stop and try to have an adult meet your child at his stop the first week of school.

If your child expresses many concerns and fears about starting school, use reflective listening skills because he may just need a sympathetic ear which gives him the opportunity to resolve his concerns. Do not say that his concerns are baseless. He may never tell you anything again.

Reflective listening requires that you listen to what the child is saying and state back to him your understanding of what he has said. If the child says: "I don't want to go to school. I have no friends there." A reflective response might be. "You feel upset because you are afraid that nobody will like you." This is an open response. It addresses the child's feelings which are very important. It gives him some feedback which tells him that you understand, and it leaves the way open for him to explore solutions.

The First Week And After

Parents very naturally want to know all about their child's school day. Give your child the freedom to choose the things which excite him about this brand new experience. Resist the temptation to go through his school bag. Do not interrogate him about school the minute he gets home. He may be bursting to tell you about the friends he made on the playground or how well he kicked the ball at soccer. Remember that school is an opportunity to learn social and physical skills as well as academic skills. You may cut off that kind of communication if you immediately focus only on academic things.

Suppose that your child comes home from school and asserts that he never wants to go back there again. Suppose he claims to be sick, and you know that this is untrue. In the past, this was called "school-phobia," and the conventional wisdom was to insist that the child return no matter what his objections. In today's world, this may be a mistake. Children's concerns should be taken seriously. Whether the underlying problem is trivial or serious, it is very real for the child. Many problems do not truly threaten your child's safety, but some do and you should be alert for them.

Ask why he does not want to go to school. You and he may be able to solve the problem quickly once you know what it is. If your child does not know or is unwilling to tell you the nature of his problem, play detective. Find out what is wrong and take appropriate action. Learn how things look from your child's viewpoint. This may require that you go with him to school and spend some time there.

If your child walks to school, go with him along his usual route. Discuss with him the things you see and be alert to his reactions to them. Sometimes a child has to pass a house where a particularly nasty dog lives, and he is frightened every day. Or he may regularly meet a group of older children who frighten him.

At school, ask permission to spend time in his classroom, lunchroom and playground. If you have time, you might volunteer to go on the first class trip or to become the "room parent." Your most important goal is find out if your child's world is unsafe. If there is nothing which really threatens his safety, look for other causes for his school refusal.

One child, after a week at school, claimed to be sick. Two days at home convinced his mother that he was using this as an excuse not to go to school. By detective work she and the teacher learned that her son feared using the lavatory which was in the classroom. The door had no lock and he envisioned another student walking in while he was having a bowel movement. The solution was to give him permission to use the boys' room in the hall which had locks on the individual stalls. This solution satisfied the child and he returned to school.

A mother came to see me because she was having difficulty every morning getting her son to go to school. After meeting with the teacher, the mother and the child, I developed a hypothesis. I suggested to the boy that he invite his mother to lunch at school, and he did. On the day of the lunch, he appeared at my office and asked, "Did you call her?" "Does she know where to go?" "You'd better call her, or she'll get lost." This confirmed my hypothesis. The boy felt that his mother was unable to function without his help. Apparently the mother said sentences like, "I don't know how I'll get through the day." "Everything's a mess." Since the boy was a concrete thinker, he took what she said literally and wanted to be home to help her get through the day. The solution was the luncheon visits. Once he became convinced that she was able to continue through the rest of the day, his fears were eased.

Another very overweight boy refused to go to middle school. Detective work revealed that the required gym shorts were too small for him and the other children made fun of him. The solution was to allow him to wear properly sized sweat pants in gym. He agreed to return to school and to gym.

While these solutions seem simple and obvious, it is important that they be found quickly. The longer the child's aversion to school persists, the more damage is done.

3

Your First Meeting with the Teacher

"Instruction begins when you, the teacher, learn from the learner, put yourself in his place so that you may understand what he learns, and the way he understands it."

The Journals
Soren Kierkegaard, 1854

Each year in school, your child is introduced to a teacher with whom he will spend the next ten months. You can and should meet this new teacher early in the school year to help her to learn about your child. Describe your child in positive terms so that the teacher is given enough information to plan appropriately for a successful year. In order to do this, you must understand your child. You need to know his temperament, his learning style, his hobbies and his interests.

Initiate a Meeting
Describe Your Child In Positive Terms
Monitor and Supplement Your Child's Program

Initiate a Meeting

Good school systems encourage parents to discuss their concerns with teachers and other school officials. You can and should initiate a conference early in the school year for any child, but especially if you have a child who always seems to be misunderstood or who has difficulty adjusting to the school routine. These are usually the children described as: "Marching to a Different Drummer."

> The verb "to educate" means "to lead", "to draw out", "to develop." It does not imply changing children into something they are not. In its highest sense, education is to take children as they are with their individual inclinations, strengths and preferences and to draw out and to develop their best qualities. Each child is unique and should be treated uniquely.
>
> The same can be said for teachers. Each teacher is unique with different teaching and learning styles and strengths. When teachers and students understand, accept and rejoice in each other's differences, true learning takes place.

Some parents take a "wait and see" attitude hoping things will be different this time around. The best strategy is to take action first. A conference is your opportunity to enlist the cooperation of the teacher by creating for your child a school environment which will enhance learning and self-esteem. It is also an opportunity for you to meet the teacher in order to understand her unique temperament, teaching style, strengths and weaknesses.

Describe Your Child In Positive Terms

When you describe your child, do so in **concrete, positive** terms. The purpose of this description is not to have the teacher change your child but to have her understand and accept him as he is. Do not talk about what he cannot do; rather describe what he **can** do, what his needs are, and how he can be helped to learn. To do this well you will need to know your child, his temperament and his learning style.

Some parents are surprised to learn that they do not know as much about their child as they thought they did.

When asked, one parent admitted that she found it difficult to describe her child's likes and dislikes. She was not sure what he would do in his spare time because he had no spare time. He had piano lessons on Monday, soccer on Tuesday, French on Wednesday, soccer again on Thursday and so on through the week. All activities structured by other people. Left to himself, what would he do? He had no time for dreaming or developing his unique personality.

In order to be able to describe your child to his teacher, you need to take the time to know him. You can learn by observing your child over a period time to discover whether he is an auditory or visual learner, sequential or systematic learner, or what is sometimes termed "right-brained" or "left-brained" learner. By observation, you can also learn about his temperament: how he perceives the world and processes information and how he relates to other people and approaches new tasks.

You might start by observing if your child learns best by the use of concrete objects like pictures and models which help him to visualize and to understand the whole concept. Or does he do better when the concept is broken down into a step-by-step, linear explanation with verbal cues. The latter type of learning is thought to be a function of the left side of the brain, and most teaching and testing in school is geared to this type of learning. The "right-brained" child, who learns through spatial relationships and who sees things simultaneously as a whole, may be at a disadvantage unless the teacher knows and accommodates to his style.

Watch to see how your child behaves. Is he very active? Does he need to touch and to manipulate objects in order to learn? Does he work best in small groups? Does he get distracted when there is too much activity and too many choices? Does he have a short attention span? Does he learn best when he can work for a short period of time and then take some kind of break? Does he like to work alone on one project for long periods without interruption?

Can you describe your child in any of these ways?

"He seems to understand everything but sometimes forgets the little details."

"He loses things and has so many interests he tends to go from one thing to another."

"He likes to know exactly what is expected of him and can memorize quickly."

All of these sentences describe how your child perceives and processes information and give you insights into his temperament.

No one way of learning is better than another, they are just different. Children learn best using their preferred mode of learning. If your child is constantly thwarted from working with his preferred style, he may not learn as well or as easily as he should. He may also feel that there is something wrong with him because he thinks and acts differently from the rest of the class. These feelings may produce rebellious behavior or cause him to stop trying. You can prevent this from happening to your child not only by understanding and accepting his style but also by encouraging others in his world to do the same.

The first meeting with the teacher is a "get-acquainted" session. You have come to describe your child and to hear the teacher's thoughts on education and children. Most teachers are interested in knowing about their students, especially if you can be very concrete in your descriptions and suggestions for what works best. You seek to understand what your child will experience in that classroom and how compatible the teacher's style is with your child's needs. You know your child best and do not be afraid to share this understanding with the teacher and to correct any misconceptions she may have.

Monitor and Supplement Your Child's Program

After your meeting with the teacher, you may find that the information you gave is not being incorporated into a meaningful program for your child. When that happens and you feel another meeting with the teacher will not bring about any changes, it may be time to supplement the school program.

If your child works best using concrete objects and the teacher only uses workbook pages, then at home you should provide opportunities to be concrete. Here are some examples.

- Take your child shopping and have him help you figure out how much things cost and use real money to pay for them.
- Build something together, perhaps a small cabinet or a birdhouse. Have him sketch out a design, choose sizes and shapes, figure out dimensions, purchase the materials and build it.
- Design your own field trips. Take him to the antiquities museum when the topic is ancient civilizations, to the county courthouse when the topic is civics, to the zoo or aquarium when the topic is biology.

If most of the school time is spent sitting in seats and being inactive, then when your child comes home provide opportunities for him to use his body. If your child likes quiet but is in a noisy classroom, provide quiet time for him to work on his own projects at home.

If your child likes to solve problems and to use logic, but the teacher emphasizes rote learning, encourage him to ask questions at home. Expose him to challenges to his thinking and reasoning. Try lots of things and find out which catch his interest. Here are some possibilities.

- "Brain Twister" books with puzzles which require reasoning to solve.
- Chess, bridge and other games in which thinking, planning and logic play a major role.
- At an appropriate age, computer programs which require mathematical and logical reasoning.

If the teacher spends more time on science than literature, then you can read poems and fantasy stories at home. If there is little time given to science, then you can spend more time at the science or "hands-on" museums that year.

If your child is not successful in any of the structured school-type activities, then it is very important that you provide an opportunity for him to be successful outside of the school. Try activities like model-building, playing a musical instrument, photography, sports, art or theater.

School systems and individual teachers vary widely in their approach to educating children. Each school year is different for your child. You need to monitor his progress constantly in order to get the best from the school, and, whenever necessary, to supplement the school's program.

A classification of psychological types developed by Carl Jung, a Swiss psychiatrist can be a tool to determine learning styles. The classifications attempt to describe how people perceive and judge the world and the relative emphasis they place on their interior and exterior lives.

In perceiving the world, **sensing** people rely mostly on their five senses. They look at the world in terms of what they can see, touch, hear, taste and smell. Students and teachers who prefer sensing stress fact over theory and reality over imagination.

Other people use **intuition** when perceiving the world. They go beyond the observable facts to possibilities, meanings and relationships. Students and teachers who use intuition favor abstraction and symbolic reasoning.

Some people prefer making judgments and coming to decisions objectively and impersonally and are called **thinking**. Students and teachers who prefer thinking analyze the facts.

People with a **feeling** style have a preference for making judgments subjectively and personally. Students and teachers who prefer feeling weigh values and are concerned about how others feel.

Extroverts like to talk and be with people, and they enjoy projects that require working in groups. **Introverts**. On the other hand, tend to keep their feelings to themselves. They enjoy privacy and need quiet time to do their best work.

4

Homework

"A man ought to read just as inclination leads him; for what he reads as a task will do him little good."

Samuel Johnson

Did you hate homework when you were in school? Did it make you a better person? How are you going to deal with your child's homework assignments?

Homework has the potential for bringing your family together or disrupting it. Since most school systems mandate nightly homework assignments beginning with first grade, it behooves you to use this activity well in order to help your child grow as a learner.

Understand the Goals and Limits of Homework
Observe How Your Child Deals with Homework
Request More Creative Assignments
Be Alert For Problems
Do Not Let Homework Disrupt Your Family

Understand the Goals and Limits of Homework

Homework, along with its role in the learning process, is an important topic for discussion by school officials, parents and students early in the school year. Homework will enhance the learning process only if its purpose is clearly understood and its guidelines agreed upon. It should be an integral part of the curriculum, not something added on in order to discipline the child.

Some schools view homework as a way to toughen the student, to prepare him to face the "real world." Sometimes homework is used as a punitive exercise unrelated to the curriculum. The purpose of homework, in this view, is disciplinary. Disciplining the mind is important, but it cannot be accomplished by giving poorly designed homework assignments. It may have the opposite effect. While you may be able to force children to do homework now, the negative backlash may produce adults who never want to open another book or to learn another thing.

The ideal result of homework should be an eagerness to pursue something independently without the constraints of a school building. In the end, homework is voluntary. It should not be something the school demands, with noncompliance punished by a poor final grade. Instead, it should be something that enhances classroom learning. The best assignments are those which your child can understand, which prepare him for class work and which encourage him to use the tools of learning he acquired in school.

There are ways to do this. Many teachers use reading assignments at home to prepare students for topics to be discussed in class. If your child comes to class with questions that he has developed from the reading, then the assignment has been successful. You, as parents, do not need to insist that he know all of the answers but should encourage his inquisitiveness.

Homework can be used to reinforce skills through practice and drill. Examples are arithmetic and spelling. Children vary greatly in their response to this type of activity. Some acquire a skill only after many repetitions, while others make it their own effortlessly. Encourage your school to be flexible in using these drills as homework. If your child has the skill, boring and repetitious assignments can only sour his attitude toward learning. Ask for alternatives more appropriate to his style.

The best assignments are those in which your child brings home work on concepts he has learned and mastered in school that allow him to demonstrate to you how much he knows. He can glow in the light of your approval. These types of assignments also give you an opportunity to get to know what your child is being taught and is learning in school day by day. One good assignment is for your young child to bring home a book he has successfully learned to read in school to read to you. Assignments in which children constantly fail in front of their parents are to be avoided. If this is happening to your child, go to school quickly and negotiate other assignments for him. A poor self-esteem as a learner is very damaging to young children.

Observe How Your Child Deals With Homework

Homework assignments which take into account the needs of the individual students are helpful. Some children need a great deal of reinforcement before they truly understand a new concept. This reinforcement can be done at home. Other children take longer to finish a classroom assignment, and, rather than miss something else in class, can finish the assignment at home. Some children love to do homework assignments and will spend many happy hours working on them. Others get very upset about doing twenty problems when they already understand the concept. Some children get confused by homework assignments and make so many mistakes that they have to be retaught the concept. Some children are perfectionists and spend two hours on a half-hour task. Others find it hard enough to sit still in school all day and find it even harder to sit still doing homework.

You should know which of these styles fit your child and act accordingly. It helps to describe your child's style to the teacher and, with your child participating, negotiate for the appropriate homework assignments.

Request More Creative Assignments

At home, parents have an advantage the schools lack. Schools are constrained by the building and the numbers of children in the class. This is why workbooks are used and photocopy sheets are given to children. To send home worksheets for children to do in isolation wastes the opportunity for creative use of the world outside of the school building.

With some thought, parents and teachers could come up with creative homework assignments that would use the tools of learning. Examples are: reading the newspaper critically and writing a comment on what was read, writing a critique on a television program, interviewing neighbors with different occupations on how they prepared themselves for their careers, writing letters to pen pals, playing family card games and doing puzzles, keeping track of the weather and weather predictions. The advantage of these types of assignments is that children are introduced to the concept of learning as a lifelong activity and not something that only happens in a school building with a teacher prompting.

Be Alert For Problems

School systems tend to leave it up to the individual teachers to incorporate homework into their programs. Some teachers never correct homework or correct it in such a way that the child becomes confused.

One first grade student had his corrected math homework sheet sent home with one answer circled in red because he had written the number 7 backwards. The student concluded that 4 + 3 does not equal 7.

You may need to check how the teacher grades your child's homework. Good work should be recognized explicitly, not just ignored. The best grading marks what the child did right rather than what he did wrong. When something is marked incorrect, the teacher should provide some guidance about what is correct. The grading should enhance, not diminish, your child's learning and self-confidence.

School Systems vary greatly on how much time they feel should be spent on homework. In Houston, concerned parents insisted that the school system limit homework to forty-five minutes a day for young children. Before this limit was set, some first graders were spending ninety minutes a day on homework. For some children, especially those with learning problems, an assignment which seemed short by the teacher's standards could be very long and frustrating for the child.

It helps if parents and teachers decide early in the school year the length of time the children should be spending on homework. The time spent should vary according to the grade level. If your child is spending an inordinate amount of time and becoming very upset, let the teacher know. An agreement should be reached about how much time is reasonable. You, the parent can confirm that your child did, in fact, spend the agreed amount of time and he should be permitted to stop, without penalty, whether the assignment is completed or not. Remember, you are your child's advocate.

Poorly conceived homework is a grave error on the part of the school because the potential is great for damaging the learning process and for creating disharmony in homes already under stress. An enthusiastic learner can quickly become an indifferent one if assignments are boring, and repetitious. Overlong assignments, not conducive to learning, can use up valuable time which children could be spending more profitably on their own creative ideas and projects. Many parents are often confused about homework and its value but feel that as good parents they should insist that their children complete these assignments no matter what. The way is paved for power struggles and anger. It can create rebellious behavior in children who fight their parents about doing the assignment.

Do Not Let Homework Disrupt Your Family

Some parents feel personally responsible when children do not do their homework. This feeling is reinforced by teachers who complain to parents when the homework is not done rather than discussing the problem with the student. It is important for parents and teachers to remember that homework is the child's responsibility. Parents can provide a quiet place for their child to work, and they can provide assistance, support and encouragement, but it is not their homework. It is their child's.

A parent's attempts to change a child's homework habits often impair the child's academic performance thus inhibiting learning. Some children do not respond well to a parent's attempt to help them and everybody winds up in a screaming match. Many times a parent's efforts are met with the sentence, "But that's not the way my teacher does it." For some teenagers, not doing homework is their only way of showing independence.

The potential for dissension is great if your child brings home an assignment involving a concept totally new and unfamiliar to him, one which has not yet been taught in school. In trying to teach him the concept, you can get frustrated and lose faith in your child as a learner because he does not understand as quickly or as well as you think he should. The child also loses faith in himself and now has the added fear that he will lose your love. This can be very damaging to the child's self image and could affect his future learning. If your child is struggling with new, unfamiliar concepts, tell the teacher what is happening at home and enlist her support to bring about a change.

One suggestion for avoiding dissension over homework is to have a time after dinner reserved for quiet, mental activity for the whole family, with the TV off. This avoids sending one child off to his room to do his homework while the rest of the family is making noise and apparently enjoying watching TV. You cannot use a "do as I say not as I do" attitude toward learning, especially learning to enjoy reading and other mental pursuits. Your children should have visible evidence that you value these activities.

It is very important for adults to remember that the purpose of educating children is to give them the tools to be lifelong learners. Any school or home activity which has the opposite effect, should be carefully scrutinized, evaluated and changed when necessary.

5

Report Cards

"A failure is not always a mistake; it may simply be the best one can do under the circumstances. The real mistake is to stop trying."

B. F. Skinner

What does your child do in school every day? What are his favorite subjects? How is he doing and does he enjoy it?

You need to know how well your child is doing in school. The school's method of reporting to you and your reaction to these reports should be supportive and encouraging to the child. Poor reporting techniques and adverse reaction of parents to negative reports can deeply damage a child's attitude toward learning.

Compliment Good Grades Rather Than Complain About Poor Grades
Emphasize Learning Rather Than Grades
Be an Advocate for Good Reporting Techniques

Compliment Good Grades Rather Than Complain About Poor Grades

Report cards can be an effective and constructive channel for communication between schools and parents. Ideally, a report card will emphasize a child's successes, and it will characterize his weaker areas not as failures on the part of the child, but as areas where the school and student will seek to do better. A growing trend is to have a portfolio for each child containing examples of his work.

Children are concrete thinkers, and grades can be confusing to them because they are abstract. When schools report what children have done wrong rather than what they have done right, children become fearful of making mistakes and avoid risks. Over concern with mistakes often causes children to make more rather than fewer mistakes and, instead of learning from their mistakes, they become discouraged. This is especially true of students who are fiercely competitive, or who set unrealistically high standards for themselves. If their excessive ambition is the result of basic inferiority feelings, then these feelings are reinforced when they make mistakes and fail to get an "A" for their work.

One kindergartner brought home his first attempt at printing the letter "a". The teacher wrote at the top of the paper, "Be Neater". Since the child could not read, he did not know what he had done wrong. He only knew the teacher was not pleased with his work. The teacher became concerned when she noticed he never took home another paper. He threw them in the basket. The teacher realized that it would have been more useful to report to the child what he had done right. She could have looked at the paper of "a's" and pointed out those that were formed correctly and asked him to make more like those.

Since it takes time and repeated mistakes to learn a new skill, schools might be more helpful to students if they encouraged the effort, graded the final product, and not the intermediate steps.

Emphasize Learning Rather Than Grades

The best motivation for learning is the pleasure in doing it. This motivation begins in elementary school and is perpetuated by parents' attitude. Since our grading system is largely based on comparing students to some standard, most of the students' motivation is to get a good grade. Many students will not take a course which offers enjoyment or challenge if they fear a mediocre grade in the course. Why take calculus and risk getting a "B" when you can take rudimentary math and be assured of an "A"? They are working for the grade not the knowledge.

You can counteract this attitude by asking your child what he learned or how he enjoyed school rather than questioning why he got a "B" rather than an "A". Try inquiring what kind of questions he asked in school that day. Children who feel pressured to get top grades sometimes will copy from others or will change their answers in an effort to cover up mistakes. Many children will deny ignorance. This can deprive them of instruction they need in order to take the next step in learning, and sabotage their future learning. They have not developed the courage to be imperfect. Children need to learn that while improvement is always possible, perfection never is. You can help your child with this by admitting that you, too, make mistakes. You can create an atmosphere in your home where it is safe to make mistakes.

Be an Advocate for Good Reporting Techniques

When your child brings home a report card which contains only uncommented grades, you learn very little from it. The only information such report cards really contain is how your child is doing relative to some often unspecified standard.

Such a report is not helpful to your child, especially when its interpretation is obscure to him. It is some secret shared only by adults. This seems strange since it is the child's learning that is being evaluated and the child is the most important person in the process. He is ultimately the one who will decide for himself whether he will or will not learn. You need to make sure that he gets clear and encouraging information. It is important that you be aware of your child's progress in school in order to encourage him, and to monitor the school program in order to change it or to supplement it when necessary.

Uncommented letter grades give you no objective information about how your child is progressing in his skills. You need this information in order to monitor his program especially in the critical skill of reading. You need to know your child's progress in reading. Do not wait an entire year to detect a problem. Interim report cards should give you the reading levels of the books he is using. If your child does not show progress in reading, it is time to request a different program for him.

One alert parent discovered that her son's reading level was not improving. She learned that, in her school system there was just one reading program for the whole school. Her son, who had hearing problems as a baby, was just not learning from this system. The school informed the parent that the only way her child could get another reading program was for him to be classified handicapped. After talking to other parents, this mother found that other children were also not learning from this program. The parents took action together, and got another reading program added to the curriculum.

You should make the assumption that your child can learn to read if taught correctly. As your child advances in school, it becomes more and more difficult for him to catch up after a critical skill has been poorly taught. In middle school, there no longer are different reading groups for different reading levels. All children are given the same books. By the time your child reaches middle school, he should be at or very close to grade level in reading.

Ideally, there should be another type of report card to help you to monitor your child's progress better. This type of reporting would be more objective and it would avoid comparisons with other children. It would inform you of your individual child's program and progress. It would present your child's reading and math levels and the textbooks currently being used. It would describe how well he uses the English language in speech and writing. It would report his capacity for higher level thinking, for example, how he integrates what he learned about science into a discussion of its effect on history. Whenever appropriate, a narrative portion of this "ideal" report would make mention of his social skills and learning style. A report like this does not have to be long or burdensome to the teacher. A few short phrases can be very revealing and helpful to you.

Learning should be a pleasant, personal, and rewarding experience for children and for their parents. You have a responsibility as parents to be well-informed so that this is the kind of atmosphere for learning your child experiences. If the school's reporting techniques damage this atmosphere, let the school know that you disagree and would be willing to negotiate another way of reporting for your child. Most schools' reporting techniques are based on their interpretation of parents' wishes. Knowing that parents want something different may help schools improve.

6

Parent-Teacher Conferences

Man's inability to communicate is a result of his failure to listen effectively, skillfully, and with understanding to another person.

Carl Rogers

Early in the school year, you met with the teacher to tell her what you know about your child. Now, later in the year, conference time has come, and it is the teacher's turn to tell you what she has learned about him. It is an evening with lines of anxious adults waiting for the parent-teacher conference. Are you ready for it? Do you know how to use it to your child's advantage?

Have Your Child Participate In the Conference
In Advance, Agree On the Agenda and Participants
Be Encouraging, Positive and Concrete
At The Conclusion, Summarize the Results

Have Your Child Participate In the Conference

Parent-teacher conferences initiated by the school are a very useful means of communication. This best occurs in an atmosphere of cooperation. When parents or teachers find conferences unpleasant or unproductive, it is time for all of them to change the atmosphere. Both groups need to work cooperatively if the student is to benefit. These conferences are even better when they are made into parent-teacher-student conferences.

Students should be part of all discussions because, in the final analysis, they are the ones in charge of their own learning. Teachers can teach, and parents can support, but if the students decide not to learn, for whatever reason, there is not much adults can do about it. Learning is not a passive activity. Students must conquer the material and make it their own.

The first thing the teacher can do to involve your child is to tell him before the parent-teacher-student conference what she plans to tell you. Your child should be given the opportunity to react either positively or negatively. In principle, what the teacher tells him should not come as a surprise. Students should know how they stand academically.

By being present at the meeting, your child gets all of the information first-hand. This also gives his teacher the opportunity to observe how he responds to you, his parent, in this situation. In turn, it helps you to learn how the teacher and your child respond to each other. If he is not involved in the conference, the teacher reports to you how your child behaves, which may or may not be the whole story, and you must report to your child what the teacher said, which also may suffer in translation. No student is too young for this. I have participated in very successful conferences with parents, teachers and first-grade students.

In Advance, Agree On the Agenda and Participants

Prior to the meeting, you and the school should agree on its time, agenda and participants. If you want a specialist such as the remedial reading teacher at the conference, that request should be made prior to the conference. If the teacher is going to have a school psychologist, social worker, learning consultant or any other member of the Child Study Team at the conference, you should know this.

If the stated purpose of the meeting is to discuss your child's academic program and progress, you should request that the teacher be prepared with samples of his work and a summary of his progress. This summary should be written if at all possible. The summary should include not only areas of concern but also areas of strength. Above all it should be encouraging, not discouraging. All adults at the conference should protect the student's self-esteem and nobody should be permitted verbally to attack the student whether he is present or not.

The purpose of conferences is for all participants to communicate effectively with each other about your child for his benefit. A successful conference involves a variety of useful skills: mediation, listening and communication. Your child can learn much from seeing these skills modeled at such a conference. If you feel insecure in any of these skills, you should seek to improve them.

It helps if you come to the conference with some questions jotted down so that the discussion can be kept directed to its intended task. It is important for you to ensure that your agenda items are addressed as well as the teacher's. Discuss this with your child in advance so that his concerns are also on the agenda. Always remember that you are your child's advocate not his adversary.

Be Encouraging, Positive and Concrete

Nobody should be permitted to label the student or speak negatively about him. If a teacher says that your child is just lazy and does not put forth any effort, it is up to you to challenge this statement and to ask for clarification or concrete examples. Such a statement is too abstract and gives no useful information. It is much more helpful if the teacher says something like, "John does not hand in his homework two of the five times during the week. Thus, he is not ready to participate in the classroom lesson on those days. This is why he is having trouble learning." This is the kind of concrete information that all parties can understand. It allows everyone involved to explore the problem and to suggest solutions.

Whenever you do not understand what is being said, or disagree with a statement, feel free to interrupt and ask for clarification or correction. This is especially true if school officials resort to incomprehensible educational jargon. **Never be embarrassed to ask that something be restated in everyday language.** If the parties in a conference consistently have difficulty in understanding each other, it sometimes helps to have an objective party present to facilitate communication.

At The Conclusion, Summarize the Results

If there are problem areas, positive solutions should have been recommended and a plan of action agreed upon. Each person should summarize his or her understanding of what conclusions have been reached and who is responsible for any action to be taken. Follow-up conferences may be agreed upon with the consent of all involved. If you and the teacher feel that a topic different from the original agenda has come up, agree to pursue it at another time.

All participants have an obligation to be constructive and positive in their approach. At the end of the conference, everyone should feel encouraged and have a sense all are working together toward achievable, beneficial goals.

Courtesy demands that you respect time schedules. Most teachers work on a tight schedule and conferences which go overtime delay waiting parents. Adults should always take the opportunity to model cooperative behavior by concluding conferences on schedule.

7

Cumulative Folders and Test Scores

"He had bought a large map representing the sea.
Without the least vestige of land;
And the crew were much pleased when they found it to be
A map they could all understand."

The Hunting of the Snark
Lewis Carroll

Most institutions keep files on their members. In school systems, these files are called cumulative record folders. Do you know that there is one for your child? Do you know what is in it? You should and it is your right to know.

Achievement Test Results
Intelligence Test Results
Comments by Teachers and Other School Officials
Problems with Evaluation Systems

Achievement Test Results

The first time you may become aware of the fact that the school has a cumulative record folder on your child is when you are given a report of standardized test scores. Most schools give these tests to children at the end of each grade. The scores are usually added to your child's cumulative folder in the form of strips of numbers for each grade in school. Some schools include IQ scores which are determined by means of pencil and paper group tests. In addition to the scores, schools may include a computer printout which separates the questions into categories indicating your child's scores in different areas.

You should understand the strengths and weaknesses of standardized tests and how schools use the scores. These tests originally were intended to permit school districts and state governments to evaluate whether or not, on average, their student population was learning and reaching the district goals.

Many school systems, with the encouragement of test publishers, now put scores to other uses which were not part of the original intent. The test results are often used to judge the individual child's progress even though they are not standardized for that purpose.

Test results are also used to judge the teacher's competence. As a result, many teachers ignore the curriculum goals established by the school and teach to the test. In these cases, the test is no longer a tool for the school to evaluate its program, it now *is* the program. You need to know what use the school is making of these test results and how this affects your child's program and progress. You also need to know what the scores mean.

Interpreting Test Scores

There are several possible ways of reporting the results to you. One is percentiles. This score ranges from a low of 1 to a high of 99. If your child scores at the 75th percentile, that means that 75 percent of the children taking this test performed below your child and 25 percent scored higher. Another way is to report grade equivalent scores. In this score, the school year is divided into 10 months and the score is expressed in terms of a decimal number with the grade before the decimal point and the number of months in that grade after it. For example. 7.8 refers to the eighth month (April) in the seventh grade. This type of scoring sometimes gives interesting results. A child in the fifth grade can get a seventh grade score in math. This does not necessarily mean he can do seventh grade math, it means he scored better than the other fifth graders taking the test. The test is only testing fifth grade math and usually does not include questions at the seventh grade level.

If you look at your child's test scores over several grades and see great fluctuations, be sure you take a look at the name of the test that is being recorded. Tests from different companies and even different tests from the same company are not always comparable. For example, primary grade tests are usually for grades first to third. The test then switches to the intermediate level at grade four. As a result, there will be a difference in scores between grades three and four. There are also statistical fluctuations in all test scores due to errors of measurement.

It is very important for you to know not only how the school interprets these scores but also what use is made of these interpretations. The computer printout of standardized test scores is only useful as a screening device to indicate a possible problem area. It is based on too little data to say with certainty that a problem exists and, if so, to identify it. If your child, for example, shows a drop in reading comprehension, you might ask if the school is going to give him a diagnostic test to determine if there is a real problem. Diagnostic tests and tests of hearing and vision give more data and help to pinpoint specific areas of difficulty.

If the school, on the basis of group end-of-year achievement tests, tells you that your child's performance is deficient in some way, you should ask a number of questions. "What further testing will be done to verify and pinpoint the problem?" "What program do you plan for my child in order to help him to learn better and possibly to improve his scores?" In other words, insist that the test scores be used as tools for planning your child's program and not merely as a statement that your child is deficient in some way.

If you doubt the validity of the scores for a particular year, ask that they be deleted from the folder. You do not need to insist on retesting. It is not very useful to subject the child to the same test again. Another kind of test, possibly one without paper and pencil, might be more revealing, especially for the child who does not test well. Some children fill in the computer-graded answer sheet incorrectly, some get distracted and lose their place, and some just freeze up. Retesting them on the same type of test will not help such problems and it does children a disservice.

Different Kinds of Intelligence

Common sense tells us and research has shown that the human mind is far more complex than data recorded in a cumulative folder. The little we do know indicates that the potential power of the brain is being used minimally at the present time. We do not even know how to define intelligence. Dr. Howard Gardner from Harvard identifies seven different kinds of intelligence:

- logical-mathematical,
- musical,
- bodily-kinesthetic,
- linguistic,
- spatial,
- interpersonal,
- intrapersonal.

How can test publishers and school systems begin to imagine that a single score can be attributed to these complex and multi-dimensional aspects of the human being?

Intelligence Test Results

IQ scores, especially those arrived at by paper-and-pencil tests, should not be in your child's cumulative folders. Such a score is not a measure of your child's native intelligence. At best, the tests measure how well your child filled in the spaces on that particular test in relation to how other children filled in the spaces. A poor test score can be very damaging to a child's future learning especially since it is not infallible, can vary over subsequent testing, and is sensitive to the child's behavior and feelings at the time of testing.

School districts that buy into the publisher's extravagant claims by making these scores part of a child's permanent record, are doing a disservice to its children. Schools should not perpetuate the myth that short answer, fill-in-the-blank or mark-the-right-space tests tell you what your child is capable of accomplishing.

Comments by Teachers and Other School Officials

You should know what is in your child's cumulative folder. It is your right, and your child's right, to know. It is helpful to view the folders during transition points: moving on to middle school and high school. **If you feel the comments do not describe your child in encouraging and objective terms, challenge them. Ask that they either be revised or deleted.**

It is interesting to see what teachers choose to say about a child. Most of the comments tell you more about the teacher than the child. Some teachers consistently write only about the students' intellectual levels, comparing them to others. Some feel that comments on the students' social development are most useful. Other teachers write more about their opinion of the parents than they do about the students.

The most useful comments, however, are those which describe your child in behavioral terms without making judgments or attaching labels. (Chapter 8 discusses labeling.)

Labeling children is not necessary and has the potential for harm. Labels give no useful information because they are too abstract. Instead, ask that your child be described in behavioral terms. Ask that the teacher describe what actually is happening, what he learned and which learning techniques worked. Here are examples:

"He knows most of his history facts, but needs extra time to finish the test and does not do well on timed tests."

"His verbal skills are good, but he has difficulty with numbers."

"He learns well in class discussions, but not as well with written assignments.

Some cumulative records are more noteworthy for the things that are left out of them rather than the things that are left in, such things as positive statements about your child's learning style, temperament, and accomplishments. You should request additions to the folder that would help the next teacher understand and plan for your child by building on his strengths.

Problems with Evaluation Systems

The basic problem with testing and evaluation systems is not only their limited accuracy but also their limited scope. They test only a subset of the full range of human capabilities. School systems place unwarranted faith in these tests. They make judgments and plan programs based on test scores. They erroneously believe that the scores can tell them what a child is capable of accomplishing. Further, they tailor their programs to the narrow set of skills addressed in the tests.

Children live up or down to our best and worst expectations. Research has shown that, when teachers do not expect much from students, that is what they get—not much. The opposite is also true. In one study, teachers were told that twenty percent of their students showed unusual potential for intellectual growth. The names of these twenty percent were chosen at random. Eight months later, these children showed significantly greater gains in IQ than did the remaining children who had not been singled out for the teachers' attention. The authors note that the change in the teachers' expectations regarding the intellectual performance of these allegedly special children had led to an actual change in their intellectual performance.

The 1988 film "Stand and Deliver" was based on a true story. It was assumed that students from a low socio-economic neighborhood could not learn calculus. One splendid teacher refused to accept that judgment. His students learned calculus and astounded the school and testing services by performing far beyond everyone's expectations for this group. At first the testing service suspected cheating because they believed more in their statistics than in the students. They insisted on a re-test, and the students proved that they understood calculus.

One of the worst fallouts from putting individual test scores in cumulative folders is that the school uses them to label children as underachievers or overachievers based on IQ scores. When a child does better or worse academically than the IQ report indicates, it is assumed that the child has done something unexpected. It is amazing that nobody calls into question the validity of the IQ score on which all of these judgments are made. The fact that the scores are never doubted gives an indication of the power these numbers have achieved in peoples' minds.

Remember that for your child the sky is the limit, given the right program and proper motivation. Anything the school does which interferes with his achieving his best should be challenged by you and alternatives offered. You are your child's advocate—the one who gives him unconditional love and support.

8

Labeling Children

"Alpha children wear grey. They work much harder than we do, because they're so frightfully clever. I'm really awfully glad I'm a Beta, because I don't work so hard. And then we are much better than the Gammas and Deltas. Gammas are stupid."

Brave New World
Aldous Huxley

"Nothing you become will disappoint me; I have no preconception that I'd like to see you be or do. I have no desire to foresee you, only to discover you. You can't disappoint me."

Mary Haskell to Kahlil Gibran
November 23, 1912

Are you aware of the labels that are put on your child? Do you do it yourself? Does your child understand what the label means and act accordingly or does he seem confused by it?

Understand the Uses and Dangers of Labels
Accept Your Child As He Is
Seek a Unique Plan for Your Child's Education

Understand the Uses and Dangers of Labels

Labeling children is a widespread practice that has a potential for harm. Any label is limiting. Society does it, schools do it, peer groups do it, and worst of all, families do it to their own children. People, instead of accepting each other as unique and worthy of love and respect, express their limited expectations in the form of labels.

"This is Joe, he's our <u>athlete</u>, and Sally, she's our <u>genius</u>."

"This is Lou, she's the <u>messy one</u>, just like her father."

"Jon is our <u>lawyer</u>, he's going to follow in his uncle's footsteps."

"Mary's no <u>brain</u>, she works hard for her A's."

"Danny never cracks a book. He's just <u>naturally smart</u>."

"Jane is like I am, a <u>math dunce</u>."

Labels adhere and for better or worse have a long-lasting affect on children's lives. They have the capacity to limit your child's potential development.

Even though labeling children is a very poor practice and is not necessary, most school systems do it. Schools require that children be labeled to make them eligible for special programs designed to meet their learning needs. The programs are valuable, but the labels are not. Ideally, the school should be permitted, without labels, to develop a unique educational plan for your child, the result of an agreement among you, the teacher and your child. It should specify how his needs for the coming year will be met. Every child could benefit from this, but, at present, only children with a handicap label receive such a plan.

A Special Case: The Handicap Label

The labels schools use can have positive or negative connotations in people's minds. Labels applied to handicapped children are often explicitly negative, and they rarely describe what the individual child is capable of doing. Examples are: communication-handicapped, perceptually impaired or neurologically impaired, socially maladjusted, emotionally disturbed, mentally retarded, multiply handicapped, visually handicapped, orthopedically handicapped and preschool handicapped. Many of these labels are medical terms and have little to do with schools.

At the present time, you may not be able to eliminate the handicap label if you want your child to receive the program he needs, is entitled to and should have. You might want to make the school know your opposition to the label, however. Let them know that you would prefer that he be put into the proper program according to his unique needs and not according to the label he has been given which does not and cannot accurately describe him.

When a label is attached to your child, it is a description of an abstract group and does not adequately describe your child or his needs in concrete, behavioral terms. Most people, however, think they know what these abstractions mean and attribute certain characteristics to a child bearing these labels. This can negatively affect the child's view of himself and his ability to learn.

Common Labels Used To Characterize Children

problem child	poor attitude
lazy	hyperactive
dull	stupid
uncooperative	inattentive
slow learner	withdrawn
star pupil	aggressive
underachieving	overachieving

When you know or suspect that labels are being applied by the school, take action immediately. Ask that your child's behavior be described objectively, and that all labels be eliminated from the school's vocabulary in dealing with your child.

Labels like gifted and talented, brilliant, and genius, which designate some kind of superiority may be just as harmful to your child as labels with negative connotations. Such labels single out a child as special, whereas he may not really feel he is special. As a result, he may fear being exposed and being demoted to a less favorable position. He may conclude that it is best to keep very quiet and take no risks which could jeopardize his position. A flattering label based on one triumph may leave him unsure of what to do for an encore. Exalted status resulting from something he regards as trivial may shake his confidence in people's judgment, or teach him that his best efforts are not required in order to be labeled special.

Accept Your Child As He Is

Do not lose faith in your child if he does not score high on tests and is not labeled "superior." Creative children are not necessarily identified by these tests. Some excel on tests because they have learned the lessons in the textbook. Other equally talented children do less well on tests because they see the problem in a different, perhaps more creative way, which does not yield the textbook answer. The maverick thinker is often unacknowledged by schools especially if only textbook answers receive the "A".

Most children who act creatively continue to do so whether or not the school's program encourages it. You can help your child most by not thwarting him. Provide him with the materials, time and space he needs to carry out his projects. For this type of child do not ask, "Did you get all the answers right in school today?" Instead, inquire, "What questions did you ask today?" A creative child will appreciate the distinction instantly. Have faith in your child as a learner and he will not disappoint you.

Seek a Unique Plan for Your Child's Education

Each child should be treated uniquely. Equal opportunity demands that each child be provided with the best program that can be devised for his unique educational needs. Teachers usually know the needs of their students. The problem is lack of resources to provide for these needs. You also know your child's needs. You should encourage your school and the agencies which support it to find the resources to meet those needs by providing the necessary programs for all children without the requirement of labeling.

9

Problem Solving

"Too often we give children answers to remember rather than problems to solve."

Roger Lewin

School, like most institutions, is not problem-free. Your child or his teacher may bring problems to your attention. Many of these present opportunities for your child to learn problem-solving skills. A few may require your intervention.

Problem-Solving Techniques
When and How To Intervene

Problem-Solving Techniques

Most of the problems which children face can and should be solved by the children themselves. You are most helpful when you teach and model good problem-solving behavior for your child. In the long run, this may be the most important tool you give him. Its development cannot be left to chance and it is **never** acquired by children whose parents solve all of their problems for them.

The first thing to do is to avoid closed responses which cut off communication. If your child says, "I hate school, and Johnny keeps pushing me." Do not respond by saying: "Don't worry, it's only the first week, next week will be better." This type of response does not help the child solve his problem and he may never confide in you again. Instead follow the steps of problem solving.

Begin by encouraging him to explore alternatives rather than giving specific advice. First clarify how your child feels about the situation: "How does it make you feel when Johnny pushes you?" It may be that your child is not angry but is sad because Johnny is the most popular boy in the class, and he wants him for a friend. You will not know this unless you ask. The next step is to help your child explore alternatives and decide what options are available to him to solve his problem. You might say: "Shall we think of some things you could do to make Johnny stop pushing you?" Try to get several ideas from your child and help him evaluate the possible outcomes of each plan. Have your child choose one idea as a course of action to pursue.

Some examples of courses of action might be: he could tell Johnny to stop it and let him know it makes him angry or sad; he could stop playing with Johnny; he could ask the teacher to change his seat; he could try to make friends by inviting Johnny to play after school at his house. After your child is committed to a course of action, let him try it and a week later, ask him how the plan is working. If the problem is not resolved to your child's satisfaction, he might want to explore another alternative. This may take more time than *your* simply stepping in and solving the problem to *your* satisfaction. It is time well spent, however, if it helps your child become an independent and creative problem solver. The child can develop a repertoire of skills so that he can successfully solve most problems he will face. Learning how to solve problems and to make decisions is as important as academic learning.

A fourth grade teacher once asked me to speak to a boy in his class because he seemed very upset and the teacher did not know how to help him. He was a good student, related well to his peers and was an asset to the group. After some questioning, the problem turned out to be that the boy and his younger brother were to be taken to a museum in New York City as a treat by the after-school program they attended. The boy felt responsible for his brother and was in a panic because he was afraid they would get lost in the museum. We tried some problem-solving techniques. First of all, we thought of the worst possible scenario. He would lose the group in the museum. What could he do if this happened? He could talk to the leader of the group and decide ahead of time where they would meet if they got lost. They could walk through this procedure to be sure everyone understood exactly where he would be. What if they still could not find him? He could call his mother in Princeton. Does he know his mother's phone number at work? He did not but he would find it out. What if he lost his money and could not use the pay phone? We then went down the hall to the pay phone and went through the procedure he could use to get the number without paying. Together, we thought of everything which could go wrong on the trip and constructed a strategy to deal with it. By the time he left, he felt much more sure of himself and seemed to be looking forward to the trip. Up until that time, he was ready to cancel the whole thing because he could think of no way to solve his problem and did not ask for help. I mention this because he was one of the brightest boys in the class academically but had not learned to use his intelligence to be a problem-solver.

When and How To Intervene

There are some problems that your child cannot solve and you may need to intervene on his behalf. When attempting to solve these problems, you can use the same problem-solving techniques you taught your child.

If your child is being physically abused, take action immediately. Make sure that the school understands that it is unacceptable. Start with the teacher. The problem should cease immediately. If not, take it to the principal. (This does not include normal confrontations with his peers which he can and should resolve himself.)

Some school systems still permit corporal punishment. If yours does, oppose it. Inform the administration immediately that you do not believe in corporal punishment and that it is not to be used on your child. It goes without saying that you should not use it as a way of disciplining your child. Physical punishment does not help a child alter his behavior, and it can destroy the parent-child relationship. You should be your child's confidant, not his adversary.

If your child is not making progress in school academically, first check for any physical problems, especially hearing or vision. A Central Auditory Test Battery may be in order. If he has auditory processing or vision problems, his program should be adjusted accordingly. If there is no physical basis for his lack of progress, request diagnostic testing in order that a more appropriate program can be put in place. Go through channels—teacher, principal and up to the superintendent if necessary.

If your child is friendless, lonely and unhappy for an extended period of time, and if problem-solving efforts have been ineffective, you may need to explore the possibility of professional help for him.

As you monitor your child's program be sure to give the teacher and school positive feedback and encouragement for their successes. If your child comes home from school excited about a new cooperative learning lesson, write a note to the teacher, with a copy to the principal and school board telling them how pleased you are with their program. If your child comes home with an innovative homework assignment or project that shows the teacher is tapping into critical thinking skills, write another note or better still, go to a school board meeting and tell the board how pleased you are. As with children, it is much more constructive to highlight the teacher's strong points rather than her deficiencies. Also, you will be viewed by the system as someone who is trying to help, not to harm.

When you do want to make a point about something which you think should be changed, put your request in the form of an "I" statement. These statements tell how you feel and how what is happening affects you. "You" statements, on the other hand, tend to place blame and make people angry. Instead of saying to a teacher, "You give too many workbook assignments and my son is not learning anything new." you might say: "I have a problem with my son doing workbook pages because I feel he does not learn as well by that method as he does by discussing the topic with peers."

Suppose you conclude that the school is seriously deficient in some respect. What should you do? First of all, assume that school officials have good intentions, and that, with proper feedback, they will make the necessary changes. Talk to the teacher first and, when appropriate, the school principal. Your attitude should be constructive. Give positive suggestions. Better yet, be willing to give some of your own time and effort to help.

If the school is unwilling to respond, or lacks the resources to do so, you may want to talk to the superintendent of schools. If this fails, try the school board. In extreme cases, it may be necessary to form a citizens committee to confront the problem. If none of your fellow citizens share your view, then you may need to seek another educational alternative for your child.

10

Judging a School System

"We thought, because we had power, we had wisdom."

Stephen Vincent Benet

In some school systems, parents can choose which school their child will attend. These parents need to know what a good school looks like to choose wisely for their child. Even if a choice is not presently available, you should be prepared in case you are given the opportunity in the future. In the meantime, you may need to take steps to improve the environment for learning in your child's present school.

How Does The School Building Look?
Does The School's Atmosphere Encourage Learning?
Do Teachers Use A Variety Of Techniques?
Is Cooperative Learning Used?
Do People In The School Act As Positive Role Models?
Are Parents Involved In School Activities?

How Does The School Building Look?

The way to start judging a school system is to take a walk through the building on a day the school is in session. The saying: "First impressions are lasting" applies to this situation.

The first thing to notice is the building itself. Observe how the building is maintained. A well-maintained old building is more desirable than a poorly-maintained new building because it usually indicates a better school system. Clean, shining buildings and dirty, poorly maintained buildings reveal volumes about the school, not only how the students feel about their school, but also how the custodians feel about their jobs. Students who are angry and frustrated take out this anger by writing on bathroom walls and destroying property. Custodians who do not feel encouraged, appreciated or recognized by supervisors and school boards take out their feelings by doing only the minimum maintenance. A poorly maintained building negatively affects all who must use it. Students get the message that they are not very important to the adults in the school.

After you notice how well the school is maintained look to see how well space is used. Is it used flexibly? Both small and large rooms should be available to accommodate a variety of activities. Classrooms should be pleasant, preferably opening out to courtyards and the outdoors. Is there a media center and library equally accessible to all the teachers and children, and is it used? In general, is the building being used in such a way that you know everyone is actively involved in the serious endeavor of educating children with joy? Or, does the use of space give you the feeling of gloom and imprisonment in a place where learning is not as important as control?

Does The School Atmosphere Encourage Learning?

Seek an opportunity to visit a classroom and learn the answers to two sets of questions:

Do the students sit most of the time at desks regimented in orderly rows? Is the teacher always at the front lecturing at the students? Are the students prohibited from talking to each other—ever? Are pencil and paper the only tools employed?

Do the students collect in several smaller groups in different parts of the room working on different tasks? Does the teacher circulate among groups? Do the children communicate with each other within the groups? Do the students work with concrete objects and tools?

These are just two ways to run a classroom, but they are not the only ways, and neither may be the best way for your child. In order to explore the full range of classroom styles, you should visit other classrooms in your district and in other school districts.

Look to see how many children are sitting outside of the principal's office for punishment. Teachers occasionally need to send a disruptive student to a "time-out" place for their mutual benefit. However, when students are consistently sent by teachers to sit outside of the principal's office as punishment, it is time for parents to take notice. Of course, the person really being punished is the secretary who not only has to do her work, but also has to supervise the "culprits". Schools which use punitive measures to force children to behave are to be avoided. Disruptive children are discouraged and need help, not public punishment. This may be an indication that this school is not an encouraging place for children.

Listen for constant announcements on the loudspeaker. These can run the gamut from giving the names of students who are the best athletes, to getting the attendance count, to a general announcement paging the principal. Too many announcement give the message that learning in the classroom is not a high priority because anything can interrupt it.

Another thing to notice is how often students are called out of classes for such things as meetings, assemblies, picture taking and so on. A certain amount of this is necessary, but some schools let these kinds of activities take precedence over what the teacher is doing in the classroom.

What will finally make the difference for your child, however, is how he will function with that particular group of children in that particular class with that particular teacher that particular year. When the total atmosphere is encouraging for everybody in the school, your child's chances of consistently having a good teacher and a group of learners in his class increases but is not guaranteed. Asking another parent how his child did in a particular class the year before is not especially useful because your child is unique and his experience will be different from every other child's. You need to monitor his program and progress continuously.

You would do that if your child were under a doctor's care no matter how great a reputation the hospital had. Do the same for your child in school.

Do Teachers Use A Variety Of Techniques?

Notice if the teachers have a repertoire of skills to accommodate the variety of learning styles found in every class. Some school systems impose the latest "innovative" program on the whole school with little input from the teachers. Some teachers respond to the new program by slavishly following its manual whether or not it fits the needs of students in their classes. Others respond by adapting the new program to fit the individual learning styles of their students.

If your child is in a new, innovative program, and he is not learning, request that the program be adapted to fit his learning style.

Good school systems encourage teachers to be flexible no matter what the program. They also train and encourage their teachers to use cooperative learning techniques as part of their repertoire.

Is Cooperative Learning Used?

The essence of cooperative learning is assigning a group goal. The teacher sets the task. The group is told the criteria that will be used to evaluate the results. The students in the group must be concerned with each other's learning, and each member of the group is responsible for knowing the work.

To complete assignments cooperatively, the students must interact with each other, share ideas and materials, pool their information and resources, use division of labor when appropriate, integrate each member's contribution into a group product, and help each other to learn. As a result, communication, conflict management, leadership and trust-building skills are developed in the students.

Cooperative group members realize that their actions affect others in the group. A student cannot sit back while others do all the work. A diversity of student ability in the group stimulates conversation among the students and forces them to verbalize. Teacher oversight of the groups in action allows for feedback to the group on their social behavior and performance and for assistance when necessary.

Mastery, retention, and transfer of concepts, are more readily acquired in cooperatively structured learning than in competitive or individually structured learning. This type of learning promotes higher quality and greater quantity of learning in addition to developing interpersonal skills. Cooperative learning lessons are also a more efficient use of classroom time.

Many teachers, convinced that cooperative learning is essential in the classroom, have had to counteract the myth that we live in a competitive world of survival of the fittest. Research has shown the opposite to be true. Hundreds of studies confirm the superiority of cooperative relationships in promoting healthy social development.

Do People In The School Act As Good Role Models?

Notice if all adults in a school act responsibly in order to be good role models for the children. If the bus driver is rude to children, and uses inappropriate language in speaking to them, then children learn that this is the way adults talk. If the cafeteria workers do not keep the cafeteria clean and pleasant, are rude to children and rush them unnecessarily through lunch, then children learn that their needs are not very important. If the secretary speaks harshly to the children and does not take time to listen to their legitimate problems, then the children learn that they and their problems are not considered important.

Opportunities for positive learning experiences are lost in these ways. Sometimes you forget that children come in contact with many adults besides the teacher in a school system. All of these adults are important in children's lives and have the potential for a positive or negative influence on them. The non-instructional members of the school community should be as adequately paid, and as carefully selected and trained as the teachers and administrators. They must know how to interact with children constructively.

Notice if staff and students speak to and about one another respectfully. Do they address each other by name as they meet in the halls and engage in the activities of the day? When students move about the halls, do they show concern for the rights of others? Is there a spirit of cooperation and respect? Or do adults cluster together in the halls ignoring the children's needs?

When you look at the school, you should see a place where everybody feels and acts encouraged. That includes custodians, cafeteria workers, aides, secretaries, students, parents, teachers, principals, superintendent and school board. They all need to feel that they are important and necessary to the smooth functioning of the school. They are all models for children, and many of the positive attributes we want our children to learn are "caught", not taught. Children are very observant and will emulate the adult models around them. A school is not a corporation with a hierarchy of power, rather it is a community of people, one of whose goals is to develop citizens who will have basic skills, who know how to learn, who are independent thinkers and who function well in a democracy.

Be alert for problems in a school system that has recently experienced a strike. Strikes tell you a great deal about the relationship between a school board and the staff. Some boards feel that their main job is to save the community money by keeping down salaries. There is a price to paid for this: a loss of trust and cooperation between the two groups.

Are Parents Involved In School Activities?

Notice if the school encourages parents to participate in school programs. Schools which welcome parents seem to benefit considerably in many ways. Parent participation enriches the school with adults who have varied backgrounds, experience and talents. It improves the adult/child ratio. Further, it provides an opportunity for constructive communication between school and parents on a daily basis. If your school does not offer them, try to get such activities started.

If you are able, you should take advantage of any opportunities the school offers which involve you in its programs. Especially, seek to be involved in those which influence school policy. Be an advocate for school councils and other forms of site-based management.

Concluding Remarks

Once, I conducted a small, informal survey by asking the question: "What is the purpose of school?" My question yielded the following answers:

- To produce responsible citizens.
- To produce thinkers.
- To develop lifelong learners.
- To protect the dreams of children.
- To teach concern for others.
- To develop all aspects of the child.
- To teach problem-solving techniques.
- To adapt to change.
- To baby-sit children and keep them off the streets.
- To keep students out of the market place.
- To produce workers.
- To help students to pass examinations.

How would you answer this question?

There is probably no single answer, but one which I would discourage is that the purpose of school is to get children **ready** for something else. Students go to nursery school to become **ready** for kindergarten. The kindergarten program makes them **ready** for elementary school. The high school program is structured to make the students **ready** to take the Scholastic Aptitude Tests and to fill out college applications. On the application a student must be **ready** to indicate he has participated in a sport, been in some community activity, been on the student council, showed independence by working at a job, taken all Advanced Placement courses and, in general, been a super-student. In its turn, the higher education system makes students **ready** for a career. As the saying goes: Life is what happens while you are planning ahead.

Somehow we have lost the sense that schooling should be an ongoing, joyful, spontaneous, creative experience, not a punitive, painful and unproductive one.

One kindergartner said to me, "Okay, I did what you wanted me to do. I learned to read. Now can I go home?" She probably intended never again to pick up another book.

You probably cannot control whether your child will become a lifelong learner since that is a personal decision he must make. You should be taking steps, however, to prevent him from being permanently conditioned against learning. The high school dropout rates indicate that this is a real possibility for many students. You can help your child by fostering a spirit of joyful learning at home and at school.

Heed the timeless wisdom on parents and children written in *The Prophet*: Be the strong and flexible bow from which your children, as arrows, take flight into the future, masters of their lives.

Things I Have Found To Be True

- Children are concrete thinkers. They cannot figure out what is expected of them if we only tell them what they did wrong. Catch them being right.
- Children who are discouraged cannot learn. Misbehaving children are deeply discouraged and do not feel they belong.
- We cannot change anybody, we can only change ourselves,
- We are all models for the children. We cannot say, "Do as I say, not as I do". Adults who are not respectful of children, cannot expect respect from them.
- Encouragement if the prime motivator. Praise is for the successes, and only a few are entitled to it. Encouragement if for the effort and we all deserve and need it.
- Accept each child completely as he is.
- Separate the deed from the doer. Never say anything against a child's person.

- Children live up to our best and worst expectations. Never label a child.
- Use "I" statements not "you" statements. Example: Instead of "You are a thief" say ""I get upset when you take money from my purse."
- Mistakes are not failures. They are how we learn.
- Rather then saying did you get an "A" say, did you ask any good questions?
- Teaching styles should vary to accommodate different learning styles.
- We cannot make anybody learn. That is a personal decision.
- Everyone in the classroom is responsible for its successes and failures.
- Cooperative learning lessons foster group cohesiveness and teach concern and respect for others.

From the Talmud: The highest wisdom is kindness.

Cassandra's Classroom

Innovative Solutions For Education Reform

Introduction

Teachers are being treated more and more like Cassandra from Greek myth. Cassandra, as the story goes, could foresee the future correctly. Her curse was that no one believed her.

I feel like a Cassandra. I have taught elementary school, grades 1-8, junior college and college courses. I have earned a PhD in educational psychology, and worked twenty years as a school psychologist. I wrote columns on education for twelve years. I believe I know the answers to the problems in education today or at least the right questions to ask. I believe many teachers and parents know the answers and the questions but only outside experts (mainly non-teaching men) are believed.

Reading these articles may give you insights which will enable you to be part of the solution and not part of the problem.

1

Teaching is a Profession

A school system could have the most modern building, the most up-to-date equipment, the most conscientious school board, the most innovative superintendent and the most caring principal but if it does not have capable teachers, it will not be successful and children will not get the best education that they deserve.

Reformers propose to improve the teaching profession by adding the rank of master teacher and by granting merit pay to a select few. The concept of a master anything is from the trades not professions. A tradesman is first an apprentice, than a journeyman, and finally a master practitioner. In a profession, for example, medicine, a person is first an intern than a doctor. There are no master doctors. If we do not believe that a person given the title of doctor has mastery of his profession, then we would not entrust him with our health care. The same attitude should be true of teachers.

We do not permit doctors to work with patients unsupervised until they have put in a long internship usually with doctors who are at the top of their professions. Minds are as important as bodies yet we permit teachers to take over a class unsupervised in many cases after only one semester of student teaching. As a student teacher, the student may not work with the teachers who are at the top of their profession. In many cases, teachers view supervising student teachers as an extra burden. The evaluation of the students is usually not done by the teachers in the school but by supervisors from the university or college the students attend.

Now is the time to initiate a change in this system, mainly because it is inadequate and does not produce the best teachers. The following is just one example of possible changes in the profession which would result in attracting and keeping the best.

All candidates would graduate from college with an academic major, not an education major. They would learn how to become a capable teacher through an internship in the school system. The candidates for an Internship would be required to pass an examination, much like the Law School Admission Test. The test would be developed not only to evaluate the candidate's academic competence but also to measure some of the qualities both personal and emotional, which distinguish the good teacher. In choosing interns, the staff of the school system should have enough information to enable them to select candidates who would enhance the diversity of the staff already in place.

The successful candidates would then enter a two-year internship in the school under the supervision of tenured teachers. Interns would be paid, and, during these two years, they would have an opportunity to discover whether they have the talent, the gift and the love of teaching necessary to be successful in the profession.

During these two years, the tenured teachers would become knowledgeable about whether the candidate should be admitted to the profession or be counseled to leave it. Many people stay in teaching even when they dislike it and are unsuccessful because they have too much invested to leave. This system allows the candidate to leave without losing anything. He still has a college degree with an academic major and a chance to pursue other careers.

On the senior teachers' recommendation, a promising intern would be offered a second two-year contract. During this period the intern would continue to work under supervision, but would be in charge of a class. At the end of these four years, a mandatory tenure decision would be made after careful deliberation by the tenured staff. These teachers would have observed the intern in the classroom and would have compiled any information needed to make the decision. In essence, it is similar to the procedure followed by university faculties.

The concept of merit pay is damaging because many deserving teachers may not get it and they could become discouraged not so much because of the money involved but because of the lack of recognition for their efforts. The competition for merit pay could consume most of the teacher's time, and it has the potential for turning classroom teaching into show business productions. What makes a teacher good is not showmanship but consistency of performance. The good teacher establishes a high level of competency and does not deviate from that level day by day and year by year. To know if a teacher is consistently good takes time. It cannot be done with one or two observations.

One of the greatest problems in education is the unevenness of the abilities of the teachers. A few inadequate teachers affect the output of the whole school and make it harder for the good teacher to function well and produce learners. Critics of education often point to these inadequate teachers and condemn the whole teaching profession. But why blame the teachers for this? They have no voice in the appointment or granting of tenure to new teachers. They did not make the poor tenure decisions: administrators did. The sad part is the administrators tend to move up and out of the school while the teachers are left to cope as best they can with these poor decisions.

The main goal of everyone connected with the school should be the optimum development and functioning of all of the staff and students. After all, schools are in the business of education. This should mean the education of everyone involved. It is a group effort, and if one member of the group fails, they all must take responsibility for this failure. In the same way, take credit for the successes. As things now stand, it is usually the principal or superintendent who is congratulated and honored for the school's successes. This seems strange when it is the teachers who are the backbone of the school system. When they are successful, we all benefit, but especially the children. Now is the time to put into place a system which will ensure more successes.

2

Attracting Competent People to the Teaching Profession

One of the problems involved in attracting competent people into education may be that it is the only profession which does not have "perks". A perquisite, according to the dictionary, is a privilege or profit incidental to regular wages or salary.

Companies pay for their employees to take courses to upgrade their skills. Many universities give sabbatical leaves of a year every seven years. Many companies routinely give cash bonuses, usually at Christmas and Easter time. These extras are not considered part of a person's salary so the discrepancy between teachers' salaries and other professionals may be greater than originally thought.

Bright young people are beginning to be attracted to the teaching profession in spite of the salary discrepancies. The problem is they will not stay because teaching is essentially a dead-end job. The only avenue for advancement is administration.

The California Commission on the Teaching Profession solved this problem in a report entitled: "Who Will Teach Our Children?" This report gave recommendations on three topics: Restructuring the teaching career and establishing professional standards, redesigning the school as a more productive workplace for teachers and students, and recruiting capable men and women into teaching. One of the most interesting parts of the report was the section entitled "The Story of a Career", in this part, the committee attempted to show how their recommendations would change the teacher of the future.

In this scenario, the teacher was paid by a fellowship program to pursue her training in chemistry. The program offered her one year of college tuition for each year of commitment to teach. She also received pay for a work-study program in which she worked as a tutor and aide in science classes in high school while attending college. As a prospective teacher, she was paid for a summer of intensive course work. At the end of this time, she took and passed competency tests to become a teacher.

She received tenure after three years and paid off her fellowship. After three years of teaching she was ready to pursue graduate work. She was able to do so because her school functioned on a quarter system and offered teachers the possibility of working on ten, eleven or twelve month contracts.

She passed a rigorous examination and became board certified. This meant a raise in salary. After several years, she received training as a peer evaluator and spent a year doing this. The next year, she returned to the classroom. She applied for the sabbatical program which allowed her to take courses for state certification as a mentor teacher and to work part-time at the research facility of a local corporation. After certification, she received a raise in salary and divided her time between her own classes and the classrooms of residents and other teachers she was helping.

She was now an esteemed educator. She served as an adjunct professor at the university, and was the recipient of professional awards. Her income, like that of other senior mentor teachers, equaled that of the school administrators. She took time off for a year to work on school-based staff development and then returned to the classroom. After twenty-five years in teaching, she could negotiate her duties each year. The district sought to use her expertise where it was most needed. She retired at 60, but continued to consult part time with the district and to serve on state-level committees.

This "Story of a Career" ended by the teacher feeling proud of her accomplishments and her life time of service. She chose a profession that offered her excitement, variety, challenge, growth in competence, income, and esteem of the community, her colleagues, and her students. Not many professions can offer those perks.

3

How Does Your School System Evaluate its Teachers

In order for your child to receive the education he is entitled to, you need to know how your school system chooses and evaluates its teachers.

A district may have award winning physical facilities, the most expensive books and the latest hot off the press innovative programs, and the smallest class size, but if it does not have good teachers, than your child's education is in jeopardy. Good school systems know this and spend a great deal of time and effort recruiting and hiring the best teachers available.

These systems appoint a committee consisting not only of administrators but of teachers and parents who have been trained to recognize the qualities they want in a teacher who would enhance the educational program in their district.

The first step the committee takes is to screen the applications of a large pool of potential candidates. They then do an intensive evaluation of the group who survived this screening.

The committee holds personal interviews with the remaining candidates and reviews their references. The review should include contacting the previous school. This review often involves talking personally to the person who wrote the reference. In the case of teachers who are recent graduates, the committee inquires about the program they were trained in, its educational philosophy and the quality of the professional staff.

When a tentative rank-ordering of the candidates has been made, the committee's next step is to start with the top candidate and to observe her teaching. The committee members have been trained to do this well. They understand that this is the most crucial step in the whole process because a teacher may talk a good line and tell the committee what it wants to hear, but have no idea how to translate what she says into working with children in the classroom.

A trained observer understands a great deal about the teacher by just looking around the classroom. Of all possible things to emphasize what does she choose? Is everything teacher-generated with no evidence of what the students are doing? Are all the desks placed in such a way that the children cannot communicate and work with each other let alone with the teacher? Is the teacher so afraid of children and of losing control that she requires complete silence and no movement?

In watching the teacher with the class, the observer has the opportunity to note how she disciplines, how she takes into account different learning styles, how she uses cooperative learning lessons, how she presents the curriculum and in general, how she functions with the group before her. This information can only be obtained by observation, not by a verbal interview. This process results in hiring the best teachers available to teach your children and is absolutely essential.

Not all school systems give rigorous, objective teacher recruitment a high priority. In some places, it is not what you know; it is who you know that counts. Those systems often have an unspoken but understood policy of interviewing and employing only those candidates with political connections. As a result, many outstanding candidates are eliminated from consideration. The children suffer the consequences of poor teaching if less capable teachers are hired. When this happens, the recruitment process is rarely blamed, rather the children are blamed for lack of intelligence or the parents are blamed for lack of involvement.

For your children's sake it is important for you to know how teachers are chosen in your district. Since many of these decisions are made over the summer, now is the time to find out.

4

Teacher Tenure

Teacher tenure laws are coming under close scrutiny, usually not in a pleasant way. One headline read: "When teachers should be expelled from class." "New hope for getting rid of bad apples". The assumption seems to be that tenure permits teachers to remain in classrooms when they are "burned out" and not helpful to children.

There must be a reason why we put teachers in classrooms with a group of children and then put these classrooms together in order to make a school. The reason should be that everyone in the school is important and that all are concerned about each other. Schools are in the business of education and that should include the education of everyone involved in the enterprise. If this is not the purpose, then maybe we should consider breaking up the schools into something more efficient. If the purpose is merely to give out information so that the children can give it back correctly in tests, then maybe a more efficient operation would be to put each child in front of a computer. If this is so, then we do not need schools at all. Each child could have a computer at home.

Most people do not believe this. Schools are made up of a community of people. Every school community must decide what it is all about and what it wants to accomplish for its members. It needs to be a group decision because each member is important for the success of the others and each member has to take some responsibility for the failures.

Any group of teachers has individual strengths and weaknesses. In a safe environment, it would be okay for teachers to say what they do well and what they do not do well. In many cases, members of the school community already have this information. They know which teachers are strong in certain areas and which teachers are not.

Teachers need to be encouraged to describe their strengths and weaknesses. This information should not be used against them, but should be used to exploit their strengths and to remediate their weaknesses.

Suppose a particular school discovers that it is weak in science and math and wants to improve. The school community knows that several teachers do not like or understand these subjects. These teachers usually compensate by rigorously following the textbooks and limiting class discussions. There are options available to the school to help these teachers.

Just to mention a few: Teachers could team teach with one taking over the science and math while the other concentrates on the liberal arts. Teachers could visit classrooms where the teachers do a great job in teaching science and math. These teachers could then become mentors to those who feel insecure in these subjects. Staff development opportunities could be made available for teachers to visit other schools with outstanding programs and report back to their colleagues about what they learned. Time and money could be allocated for some teachers to take additional courses in a highly recommended science and math program. In other words, they would be helped to succeed in this educational enterprise called a school.

The may sound too "pie in the sky" to be practical but it is more practical than having a complex, expensive program of recertification which probably will not result in changing teachers or education. There has to be a more fundamental change in the system which would have a domino effect to bring about other changes.

The change necessary would have all the occupants of the school responsible for everything that happens there. This also includes the students in each individual classroom. Children are not in classrooms merely to interact individually, one-on-one with the teacher. They are part of a group brought together to help each other to learn and to grow. The same thing should be true of every adult connected with the community called school.

5

The Role of Administrators in Schools

I once heard of a Symphony Orchestra whose members hired the conductor themselves and kept him as their conductor as long as he helped them to produce outstanding music. If the conductor became unable to bring out the best the orchestra had to give, they fired him. In other words, the conductor's job was to make them sound good, not the other way around. The same thing should be true of schools. The principal's job and the superintendent's job should be to make the teachers look good. Not the other way around.

The most prestigious position in education should be that of the teacher, not the principal or any other administrator. The principal ideally should be a Master Teacher chosen by the teachers he or she is to lead to better teaching. The principal should be a person of proven ability and experience who sets an example, knows how to monitor and to counsel teachers and helps them to reach the high expectations they have for themselves and their students. The principal's function should be to inspire, to motivate and to direct the staff. The ideal relationship between the principal and staff would have the principal first among peers, responsible to them and an advocate for them.

Some school systems contend that a principal does not need exposure to classroom teaching in order to function well as principal. Is the principal to be the educational leader of the school or simply a business manager whose main job is to see that supplies and services are made available within the school budget, schedules are met and forms properly filled out? A person serving in the role of principal could function adequately with only administration and management skills. However, such a person is a business manager, not a principal.

It is time we recognize that the role of principal involves two different functions. one of professional leadership, the other of administrating services. These functions might best be served by separating the one position into two. The more important and most prestigious function should be that of professional leader. It is the role that requires more training and experience and therefore higher pay. The person administrating services, however, could have many schools under his or her jurisdiction. This is a more cost efficient way to administer schools since materials bought in volume become cheaper.

Also, since most state and federal forms and requirements are the same for the district, it seems more efficient to have just one person to deal with them. This person would also oversee the buildings and grounds and in general be doing what needs to be done, within fiscal constraints, to carry out the mission defined by the educational staff. The principal and teachers should give their full attention to the main function of education: students' learning.

6

Making the School Building
an Educational Enterprise

A twelve-month school year has the potential for bringing about many positive changes in a rigid system. One thing that would have to change is the use made of the school building. Other changes occur as teachers confer with each other and exchange ideas.

School buildings have traditionally been shut down during the summer months. This is vacation time for the staff. Normally, it is impossible to work anyhow in most of these buildings because they lack air-conditioning. During the school year, buildings are usually open from 8AM to 4PM. All of this could change if schools began to function on a twelve-month schedule. School facilities could be used to their fullest.

School buildings should be known as educational centers and be available for the educational enterprises of the whole community. The school building should be available to the community from 6AM to late in the evening, six days a week from January to December. This would require upgrading most schools not only by adding air-conditioning but also by reconfiguring space to make it more adaptable for use in different activities and by various group sizes. As things now stand, the buildings are under-utilized. The equipment, books, supplies, and material in most buildings are only used for short periods of time. Most material is discarded because it becomes obsolete rather than worn from use. Equipment is usually kept in individual classrooms and when the teachers are not there, the rooms are locked and the material sits unused.

Instead of each classroom having its own equipment, a more useful concept is a media center. The Media Center, including the Library, would house the VCR equipment, TVs, computers, books, and other materials necessary for the educational endeavor. Like the kitchen, cafeteria and gym facilities, it should be easily accessible to everyone in the building. In this way, maximum use is made of everything in the building on a year round basis.

The Educational Enterprise should be available for all ages. Pre-School children and children whose parents work should have access to it as early as 7AM and should be able to stay until 6PM. Children who require an after-school program would remain in the building under supervision of that program' staff. Senior citizens could make use of the building at times when space becomes available. When senior citizens begin coming to the Educational Building, the opportunity is available for them to see ways in which their particular skills would be helpful to the staff and the students. The offices of administrators should also be in the Educational Building. Sometimes administrators get so far away from students that they lose contact with the real world in the schools and become less effective.

Schools open all year could be reorganized for more flexibility in planning not only teachers' schedules but also students' schedules. The vacations of the students and teachers could be staggered over the year in order to make full use of the school facility.

The way is also open to reorganize the structure of classes and discard grade designations. Since the school is open twelve months, it would no longer be necessary to have the first grade, second grade and so forth. The present grade system divides time into blocks and some children fail because they cannot keep to this rigid pre-determined schedule. A better system involves individualized programs in which children advance when they have achieved mastery. Acknowledgement would, therefore, be made of differences in maturation rates, interests and learning styles.

With a twelve month school year, teachers will have time to confer with each other to consider more flexible ways to use their time and talents. Teachers, who feel comfortable with the team teaching concept, might try an arrangement where two teachers are responsible for one class. One teacher comes in the morning and the other comes in the afternoon. This type of arrangement is convenient when teachers want to have time to take courses, to observe and to train interns, and to attend professional workshops. When one teacher is out, the other teacher takes over. This and other types of arrangements guarantee continuity of instruction to the students and give the teachers the flexibility needed to accomplish their goals.

Another way to achieve flexibility is to have a group of children assigned to several teachers for a period of years or to have one teacher continue with the class. A school of 2000 children from grades five to high school in Cologne, Germany uses this system. Eighty-five to ninety students are assigned to a team of six to eight teachers. The students never experience a substitute teacher. All of the decisions are made by this teaching team: how the students will be grouped; which teachers will be assigned to which students; who will teach any subject and how many subjects will be taught each day. In addition, this team of teachers remains with the same students for six years.

When teachers are given the opportunity to communicate with each other over educational issues, they have the possibility of attempting new and potentially more successful teaching strategies. The teachers in Cologne decided to use the technique of cooperative learning in their classes. Pupils work in groups of five and six and are of mixed ability levels. There is a minimum of teacher talking and lecturing. Students are actively engaged, working on problems together, helping and learning from each other.

Another group of teachers restructured the curriculum and began the Key School. These teachers decided to tap students' multiple intelligences through the use of an interdisciplinary curriculum. The curriculum they developed is tied together by themes that span all grades and subjects which change over the course of the year. In addition the students receive instruction in the basic academic subject. These teachers not only are using their gifts and creative talents for the good of their students, they are making teaching an exciting, vibrant and involved profession.

The introduction of the twelve-month school year has the potential for bringing changes in a rigid system that finds it difficult to change. It will cost money, of course, but so do military weapons, bail-outs of financial institutions and other changes.

Now is the time for change. Our children deserve nothing less than total commitment on our part.

7

Who Decided?

Who decided that the concept of middle school for children from ten to fourteen was a good idea? At the very time when children are most insecure, they are forced to leave a familiar environment where they know the teachers, their classmates, and the school to go to a new school in which they have to begin all over again.

At a time when children should be able to contribute to the school community by being leaders and top of the heap, they are made insignificant by being put at the bottom of the heap.

They are forced into a situation where they have to re-establish themselves with a group of new students, new teachers, new rules, and lots of anxiety. At this most precarious stage of their development, physically, mentally and socially, the school system gives them a double whammy by casting them adrift.

Who decided that the K-8 school was an outmoded concept and children needed to be separated from younger children when they reach preadolescence? In the K-8 school, the older children were leaders the younger ones looked up to and wanted to emulate. The K-8 school helped the older students by putting them on the student council and in general gave them opportunities to become responsible models for the younger ones. The school also crossed age lines and used older students to help younger ones to learn. Older students understood that they should not disappoint the younger ones by acting irresponsibly. It would be noticed because everyone knew them and had high expectations.

Who decided that middle school teachers could teach any subjects because they had a K-8 certification? If they are assigned to teach math, science or social studies, they do not need any extra certification in these subjects as do high school teachers. Many schools do not provide teachers with extra training when they make these assignments.

There are a lot more questions that come under the topic of "Who Decided?". Who decided that the school year should consist of 180 days out of a possible 260 days? Who decided that children should be segregated by chronological age rather than by other criteria such as: ability level, maturation level, learning style, to mention but a few? Age probably is the least valid indicator of the range of possibilities of a group.

Who decided that there is only one way to teach a subject and that administrators are the best judge of what that method should be? The whole language approach to reading as opposed to phonics is one example. Instead of teachers being expert in several approaches, they must teach one approach, and if the child cannot learn that way, he fails. No consideration is given to the fact that children have different learning styles: some are right brain learners, some are left. Some require a great deal of repetition and hands on experience, others do not. Some are auditory learners, others are visual. Some are slow to mature, others are not.

Who decided that administrators and school board members are better judges of what makes a teacher good than the teachers? Administrators and Boards give teachers life-time tenure then leave and the teachers and the school are left with the consequences of their ill-formed, often politically motivated decisions.

Who decided that teachers are qualified to practice their profession with a few months of student teaching and no internship? At least three years internship under the guidance of experienced teachers should be required before a new teacher is left on her own in the classroom.

Who decided—but I am running out of space. You can add your questions now.

8

Two Year Diploma

Students need to have some say in their education.

I would like to propose a use of vouchers and a two-year diploma in public education which would solve the problem of the dropout and the disruptive student.

Perhaps we are dragging the whole process out longer than is necessary or healthy. Mortimer Adler says adolescence is a pathological state, half way between being immature and being mature. Also today's children become physically mature at an age earlier than the previous generation. Suppose we shortened the whole process to two years of high school. The requirements for the diploma would change but after two years students could leave with a certificate. The next two years could be more like a junior college program.

The diploma would certify that the student can read, use correct English, knows how to verbally communicate, can write clearly, can negotiate: understands finances and basic mathematical concepts, and knows how to be a good citizen. Since he is entitled to four years of schooling, he can choose to go further, to learn a trade, be an apprentice for two more years or choose college prep courses.

When I was a counselor at a junior college in California, all students over eighteen were admitted with or without a high school diploma and it was free. There was more prestige in attending college than high school. The catch was that they had to pass tests in math and English as a prerequisite for other courses. They took remedial courses until they passed the tests. Many students never got past the remedial courses mainly because they had not used their time wisely in high school where they had been truant, unruly and often suspended. There was never a discipline problem in Junior College because they were there by choice, not by law.

Schools are places of learning for those students willing and able to learn. There is an implied contract. Teachers can teach but it is up to the student to learn. If the student, for whatever reason, is not ready to learn, then the contract is broken. Schools were not meant to be punitive institutions or holding pens to keep disruptive students off the streets.

The system could change with the use of vouchers. If a student wants to work and sees no advantage to attending school, his voucher would be returned to him to be used at a later date. If a student is disruptive and is not taking advantage of the education offered, his voucher could be returned to him to be redeemed at a later time when he is ready. The students are not labeled dropouts and they are not being punished. They are making a choice to defer their education to a time when they can profit from it.

With this system, schools get out of the business of being punitive. Students who drop out of school do not need to be labeled or punished. They are already punishing themselves by their self-destructive behavior. Instead, the students make the choice and they have a say in what happens to them. The schools merely let the consequences of the students' behavior take effect. At the same time, schools leave them with hope for the future. The opportunity is always there for them to redeem their vouchers at a later date in order to rectify a mistake they made when they were very young and very immature.

Schools may need to become more accessible in order to accommodate a different population of students under this plan. Many will be older and take longer to complete a program. Many will be working and, perhaps supporting a family. Schools would need to be open twelve months a year from morning through evening to accommodate all students.

When the student chooses to learn, at whatever age, he should find a welcome at the school and a curriculum appropriate to his needs as a learner. This use of vouchers is encouraging and positive to all students. Why not give it a try? A successful democracy requires that all its citizens have the education necessary to make informed decisions.

9

Uniform Approaches Nose Out Individuality

Many years ago my friend went to Hollywood to have plastic surgery done on her nose. She felt her nose was too big and she wanted movie star, Kim Novak's nose. That is what she got because, at the time, this was the ideal nose and every woman who had plastic surgery got the same nose. While my friend's new nose was smaller, it did not improve her looks which had been striking. It just made her look like every other woman who had Kim Novak's nose.

Outstanding plastic surgeons no longer do this. The object of the surgery now is to improve the unique looks of the individual person and not to make that person look like somebody else. When the surgeon is successful, people do not notice that the person's features are different; they just notice that the person looks rested and wonderful.

Plastic surgeons learned something very important. They did not have to make duplicates of some perceived ideal face, which would be boring; they could work with the face each person brought to them and improve it without changing its uniqueness. Schools could learn a lesson from this.

Each child who enters the school system is unique. Children are more unique and creative as kindergartners than they are as seniors in high school. As kindergartners, each one has a unique way of looking at problems, at solving them, at asking interesting questions, at viewing events and the world around them. They have taught themselves a great deal in five short years and arrive at school as accomplished learners, interested and curious. Most school systems, however, instead of building on this uniqueness and treating children as individuals, proceed to fit them into a uniform mold.

Schools have decided what and how a child will learn before they ever see him. Schools have a pre-determined curriculum, time-table, and evaluation schedule.

Each child gets the scholarly equivalent of Kim Novak's nose, the standard model for education. As in the case of the surgeon, who eliminated my friend's beautiful nose, the school eliminates a unique creative way of thinking in order to provide the standard model. One cannot help wonder if inept plastic surgeons, like poor school systems; give their clients Kim Novak's nose because that is the only nose they know how to make. Is it because they do not know another beautiful nose when they see it. Or could it be that they really do not want different models but clones because they are easier to handle and to categorize.

School systems, by the early introduction of workbooks, worksheets, and other fill-in-the-blanks type of learning, quickly eliminate individuality and creativity in children. Instead of rewarding imaginative questions, the school wants only the right answers. There is only one answer that goes in those blanks. Young children quickly learn the drill and stop asking questions which are not in the curriculum. One researcher noted that tests of creativity were not valid after the third grade because children no longer thought or solved problems differently. They had become clones of the standard model. Of course, this may be what schools want to produce because they and their programs are going to be evaluated by clone-type tests.

I am not sure what made the plastic surgeons realize that they should change and not give everybody the same face. Did they just become wise by themselves or did their clients become smarter and demand something different that forced them to change? Maybe we could do the same for our children. Informed parents must demand what is best for their unique children.

10

Schools' Programs No Excuse For Failure

I once worked with a student who I discovered had a disability in spelling. He seemed relieved when I told him this. He had felt stupid because he could not spell no matter how hard he tried to memorize the words.

Later, he showed me a composition he had written in which many words were spelled incorrectly. I asked him why he was handing in a paper with misspelled words in it. He replied that since now everyone knows he has a disability in spelling, nobody should expect him to spell words correctly anymore.

I informed him that is not how it works. Knowing he has a problem with spelling is information he must use to solve his spelling problem. He no longer has to feel dumb or defensive about his disability, but he does have to find ways to compensate for it.

He may have to look up every word in the "Bad Spellers Dictionary" when he is unsure of its spelling. He may have to use "Spell-Check" on a computer. He may need to do many things to compensate for his disability, but he may not use it as an excuse for poor spelling.

The same reasoning is true for schools. Schools now know that many of today's children are born in poverty, are abused, and or live in homes which are not intellectually stimulating. Such children come to school in poor health, with short attention spans, poor motivation, are behind their peers intellectually, and are passive learners.

Just because everyone is aware of these deficiencies, that does not mean that schools can use this information to justify their failure to educate these children. They probably cannot be taught using the same methods which work for children coming from supportive home environments. They can learn, however, with encouragement and the right programs.

Many people believe that the present educational system is adequate as long as the requisite familial and social supports are provided for the students outside of the school. They conclude that where the supports are lacking, the system does not have to change; the families do.

For complex sociological reasons, many families are unable or unmotivated to function differently. Their children, through no fault of their own, suffer the consequences of these non-existent support systems. Schools that cling to educational programs inappropriate for these children join the ranks of failed support systems.

This type of thinking allows schools to do what the boy with the learning disability did. That is to perpetuate the myth that they are not responsible for deficiencies not of their making. It is true that schools are not responsible for the deficiencies but, like the poor speller, they must use knowledge and understanding to overcome these deficiencies.

One example was a recent description of what happened to a Chicago school system in the suburbs when white students fled from the neighborhood. One social studies teacher was quoted as saying that the school declined because blacks moved into the neighborhood. He says they won't shut up in class, so now he relies on videos to do the teaching for him.

There was no indication of how he would change his style of teaching in order to reach the students in front of him. This particular teacher will not change, he will just bide his time until retirement.

If the poor speller does not develop strategies, the result will merely be misspelled words. If the school systems and teachers do not develop strategies, the result will be another generation of children condemned to poverty and ignorance.

Schools are the last hope for those children whom society and their families, for whatever reason, have failed. School systems have the potential with our encouragement and our support both financially and emotionally, to succeed where other systems have failed. We must give the children and the schools that support now.

11

Everything I Wasn't Ready to Learn in Kindergarten

When a child enrolls in kindergarten and becomes part of a school system with all of its rules and regulations, parents suddenly feel left out of the decision-making process. Well parents are not the only ones, it turns out. Sometimes teachers feel the same way, especially kindergarten teachers.

At one time, the teaching of reading was not permitted in kindergarten and there was a special early childhood development certificate required for kindergarten teachers. Now any teacher, many with little or no training in early childhood development, can be assigned to kindergarten. As a result, and much against the early childhood educator's advice, kindergarten programs now emphasize reading, workbooks, testing, group drill, fill-in-the blanks and color-in-the picture activities. These teacher-directed activities tend to inhibit young children's creative impulses and much of this activity is developmentally inappropriate.

The trained early childhood educator would begin her year by taking the time necessary to get to know the developmental levels of her students before introducing pre-packaged programs.

She would introduce appropriate programs only when her students had achieved a level of readiness to be successful. To achieve this level, she would spend time providing opportunities for the children to increase their socialization skills, their expressive and receptive language skills, their creative talents. She would provide access to play centers, like a store, a house or a dress-up corner, and lots of opportunities for creative art and music activities.

She would take the children on trips to the firehouse, the store, the library, the farm so that they could come back to the classroom and talk about their shared experiences. She would read and discuss stories with them. She would involve them in a great number of hands-on activities, like using different-size measuring cups to play with water. They would be able to play with sand, to sift it to feel its consistency, to make designs with it and perhaps to trace the first letter of their names with it. They would be planning and planting a garden. All activities about which they can talk, and draw something and perhaps make a class story which the teacher writes for them.

If your child seems to be upset and not enjoying kindergarten, you might talk to the teacher and explain what is happening to him. He may not be developmentally ready to be successful at the task he is asked to do. When he is ready, he will do well on the same tasks he is presently failing.

It is important to know the school's curriculum in order to supplement it or to do something different at home if you disagree with its philosophy or pace. Instead of teaching your child the alphabet or how to count to 100 at home, try to talk, to listen and to read to him. It will be time well spent since all children do better when they have a strong foundation in language.

When your child first comes home from school, do not quiz him about his academic accomplishments and go through his bag to examine his school papers. Rather, ask: Did he make a friend that day? What did he build in the play corner? What did he talk about in school? What was fun? Did he ask any questions?

Parents can best help their children by acknowledging that children mature at different rates and the rate of development is not correlated with intelligence. Parents and teachers who attempt to accelerate this rate are doing children a disservice and causing them unnecessary stress. Remember, childhood is a journey, not a race.

12

Life Long Learners

The purpose of education is not to produce students who do well on standardized tests but to produce life-long learners who enjoy learning and are successful at it. In order to accomplish this goal, children not only need to be taught the tools for learning they also need to be taught how to use these tools so that they can continue to learn with or without the supervision of adults, in or out of school. As one kindergartner put it, "I've learned how to read, now can I go home." She probably never planned on opening a book again. She had been turned off by the whole process.

Children take different roads to learning. Some go quickly, some slowly, some are right-brained thinkers some are left. No one way is better than another. They are merely different. These differences need to be recognized and accepted. Children need not be separated from each other because of these differences. If we do that, we have what Bruno Bettelheim called, "Segregation, New Style." Children need to learn how to appreciate and negotiate with all styles of learning. They need to be exposed to the experience of hearing a topic discussed and thinking, "How interesting. I never thought of it that way." At the same time, different styles and rates of learning among children should not hinder their development or their potential for creativity. We need to develop workers for the whole spectrum of jobs in our country from creative leaders to creative craftsmen. How can we do this given our diverse population? One way is to recognize that there are several types of teaching in elementary school. One type includes basic skills: reading, writing and math. Another involves the acquisition of concepts and the analysis and exchange of ideas as in the humanities, the natural and social sciences. Children can be divided into groups according to learning style and rate of learning when teaching a skill, then brought back together as a group when using the skill as a tool for learning. For example, it makes sense to break up the class into homogeneous groups according to skill level when teaching reading, but to have heterogeneous groups for cooperative learning lessons.

This philosophy holds true for gifted and talented programs. Children in the best of these programs, instead of being completely segregated, spend time with other children. However, the distribution of their time can be different. Gifted children need less time acquiring skills and learning facts and more time exchanging and analyzing ideas. They can spend some time with all of the students learning how they think and arrive at conclusions and being contributing members of this group and some time with a small group of select students like themselves. It helps also to remove the top students from the group at times because it allows the next level of students a chance to be on top.

Many children are spending most of their time at the knowledge level of learning. That is they are learning to label, to repeat, to reproduce, to list and to describe. Most students will forget this information quickly because it is not put to any practical use and is never applied or used as a tool. We want more for our students. We want them to be creative critical thinkers who use what they are learning to further their knowledge and to solve problems and answer their questions.

13

True Reform

Results from the New Jersey Collegiate Basic Skills Placement Test and the Scholastic Aptitude Test indicate that not only are students not improving their performance, they are regressing. Obviously educational reforms, at least in New Jersey, are not working. The reason may be that true reform does not show instant results but takes time. True reform requires a top-to-bottom overhaul not merely applying Band-Aids on failing practices already in place. Current inadequate practices have enormous inertia and are almost impossible to change.

True change gets at the root of the problem and does not merely attempt to treat the symptom. There are three places where change needs to occur to get at the root:

1. Child care programs which nurture the physical, intellectual, social and emotional development of the child from birth to age three.
2. Teacher education programs which encourage, train and nurture young people who have the desire, ability and temperament to be outstanding teachers.
3. School choice programs whereby schools give up monopoly protection which mitigates against change.

Changes in these three areas are difficult but not impossible. The good news is we do not have to start from scratch or re-invent the wheel in order to accomplish these changes. The research studies have been done and we know what works. Other countries and other states have begun to incorporate these findings into programs which are successful.

All that needs to be done is for our state to follow the leaders to help all New Jersey children as other states and countries are helping their children.

Let us start with day care. We can look to France for that program. France believes that children are a national resource and are everybody's responsibility and that the day care system is to help children to develop and thrive. There is mandated paid parental leave for childbirth and adoption. All day care providers are licensed, and receive benefits like sick leave and social security. Day care programs are visited periodically by trained pediatric nurses. Teacher turn-over is low and the providers receive good salaries and subsidized training. We have far to go to meet France's standards. Further delay can only make the task more difficult.

When children are nurtured from birth, they come to school enthusiastic, curious, creative and ready to learn the school's curriculum. They should expect to have teachers who know how to nurture these qualities. Otherwise what has been a good beginning can have a tragic end. Poor pedagogical practices produce dropouts.

Arthur Wise, President of the National Council for Accreditation of Teacher Education, gives only one example: forty percent of our math teachers did not major in math and are not certified to teach it. Most colleges require that teachers take disconnected "how to" courses, in many cases taught by professors who are not themselves master teachers. Many teacher training programs do not have a vision of the kind of teacher they want to produce and do not have a thoughtful philosophy of education based on research and sound educational practice.

Research has shown us what is needed to make our schools work for our children. It is time the citizens of New Jersey and the United States take action to demand that changes be made which get at the root of the problem. We have failed many students of this generation. Let us try to do better by the next.

14

Childhood

Schools and parents need to understand how children grow and develop in order to provide the best learning experiences for them. These days, most parents and schools emphasize only the cognitive development of the child. The physical, emotional and social development is not considered as important and is usually ignored even though these aspects of the child's development cannot be separated from the cognitive.

Given this trend, however, one would assume that since so much emphasis is being put on the cognitive development of children that educators and parents know what they are doing and are doing it well. This does not appear to be the case. What is actually happening is that adults are making mistakes because of this misplaced emphasis and are even forgetting some things about a child's learning that they used to know. It seems that the time is ripe to review the results of the research conducted by Dr. Jean Piaget on the cognitive development of children. He is the author of many books including "Science of Education and the Psychology of the Child."

Professor Piaget worked at the Institute Rousseau in Geneva. For much of his career, he studied one limited area of life, i.e. the spontaneous growth of the capacity for logical thinking. His concept of intelligence is biological. He believed that man, at birth, is less equipped with innate mechanisms than any other living being. This forces each person to go through a process of development which can only be done by acting on and reacting to the environment. Developing babies rapidly learn to influence their environment, to adapt it to themselves and to learn about it by exploring it. This exploratory drive, sometimes called playfulness, has a direct bearing on how the child learns.

Childhood, therefore, is not a necessary evil, but is a biologically useful phase in which the child adapts itself to a physical and social environment. Every child must experience his environment in order for learning to take place. Piaget found that children must progress through a series of stages before they attain adult intelligence. These stages are the same for everybody and a stage cannot be skipped. He believed that, if a developing person fails to complete a stage, further progress is inhibited.

Adults tend to want to get on with it and to rush children through these stages. Sometimes children are given activities which, while harmless, may be nearly useless at their stage of development. Hans Furth, a student of Piaget and author of "Piaget for Teachers", feels that the average five year old is unlikely, when forced to practice reading or writing, to engage his intellectual powers to any substantial degree. Other, less abstract activities are more appropriate to that level, and more likely to stimulate those powers. In Furth's view, the Educator's role is not to treat the child as an ignorant adult to be stuffed with facts, but to remember that the child's mind is growing and developing. The child should be provided with opportunities to form his own intellectual and moral reasoning powers by interacting physically and socially, as well as intellectually, with his environment.

In J.M. Stephens' book, "The Process of Schooling", the following proposal is made: Adopt the model of agriculture for schooling rather than that of the factory. The "factory educator" looks at schooling as an assembly line and expects that, for every innovation on the instructional assembly line, some measurable effects should appear in the product, i.e. the students coming out. In agriculture on the other hand, you do not start from scratch, and you do not direct your efforts to inert and passive materials. You start with a complex and ancient process, and you organize your efforts around what seeds, plants and insects are likely to do anyway. You do not supplant or ignore these older organic forms, you work through them. In like manner, our children embody a miraculously successful strategy of nature which we must not ignore.

What is needed is considerable sensitivity and common sense. Rousseau taught us, "Hold childhood in reverence, and do not be in any hurry to judge it for good or ill . . . Give nature time to work before you take over her task, lest you interfere with her method . . . A child ill taught is further from virtue than a child who has learned nothing."

15

Geniuses

Are we producing any geniuses? Geniuses are risk-takers. They put novel ideas together and see what happens. They do not seem too concerned about coming up with the "right" answer. Rather they ask the question: "What if . . ." They have not lost their child-like curiosity.

Before entering the school system, children ask lots of questions. "Why is the sky blue?" "Where do the stars come from? And why do they twinkle?" "Why does three times four equal four times three?" are just a few. Most parents can add to this list other thought-provoking questions asked by their children.

The school curricula tend to retrain children not to ask their own questions but to learn answers to the questions asked by adults. Geniuses seem to have the capacity to ignore traditional questions and to come up with new questions and their own unique answers.

There are ways for you to help your child to continue to be a questioner. Encourage but do not force your child to make the most of each impulse of curiosity. Provide a stimulating environment without the pressure to achieve. When your child expresses curiosity about something, try to gauge the depth of his interest and provide appropriate books, tools or other means for him to continue his quest to know. Then get out of his way. Do not make it your project. Curiosity should be natural, not forced. When it is forced or the child is made to feel that he is doing something unusual, the impulse may leave him.

There are children who develop specific talents early and become labeled as prodigies. These children sometimes have a difficult time as adults because their talents, while unusual in children, are not so unusual in adults. They may have become true geniuses as adults had they not been labeled exceptional at a young age.

John Stuart Mill's father brought him up to be a risk-taker and original thinker. In his autobiography, Mill says that his Father never allowed anything he learned to become an exercise in more memory. Anything he could learn or find out by thinking he was never told. He was only told when he had exhausted all efforts to find the answer himself.

The autobiography of the physicist, Richard Feynman, talks about how his father educated him. When they went for walks, his father never had him memorize the names of all of the trees and plants, rather he asked him to describe what he saw with his eyes and what he felt with his own senses.

A study of children who were exceptional in math found the following characteristics: they were quick to generalize; they were flexible in their thinking and could change easily from one process to another; they were not bound by techniques that had been successful in the past and so could change to other techniques when these failed; they looked for simple, direct, elegant solutions; they could easily reverse their train of thought.

Think of your child's school program. Is it helping him to become this kind of creative thinker? If it is not, you might want to provide the appropriate atmosphere in your home. Such an atmosphere should help him to develop those characteristics which are useful not only for traditional academic skills but for handicrafts, the arts, the trades and daily life.

A child is never helped by being pushed to do things before he is developmentally ready to do them. Rather, he is helped by being encouraged to ask questions both at home and at school and to have his questions acknowledged. He is helped by being encouraged to be curious about the world about him. He is mostly helped by being encouraged to be an active learner and not just a passive observer.

If you have nurtured your child to become this kind of learner and thinker, you should monitor his school program to ensure that what you have begun continues.

Finally, good teachers require school systems which encourage and nurture their talents.

16

Special Education

The law states that in order to serve the needs of special education children there must be a Child Study Team available to every school. The core team members include a school psychologist, a learning consultant and a social worker. Three highly trained people in complementary disciplines.

The school psychologist has the expertise to develop programs both for staff and students that would deal with situations before they became problems. The learning consultant has the expertise to work with students and staff to enhance the learning process. The social worker has the expertise to work with students and staff to promote social awareness among and between groups. All of this training and talent is going to waste because special education is overwhelmed with rules and regulations.

There are only two things most child study team members have time to do under the law: test and fill out forms according to a rigid schedule. These required tasks take up so much time that there is none left to make even these activities meaningful.

Bureaucracies only believe in numbers. They really do not care what the numbers mean or what use is made of them. They want everything documented and reported. The resulting reports go in a file and stay there because there is no time for anybody to look at them and really understand them.

Bureaucracies trust nobody to act competently. Members of child study teams know what programs are good for children. They do not need to do exhaustive mandated testing or to assign labels to know this. They need only to work out appropriate programs with competent teachers. The most thorough testing, the most beautiful reports, the most wonderful recommendations are pointless without competent teachers.

It is not necessary to second guess the capable teacher by constant evaluations of the child. After the child has been in the class over a period of time, the teacher knows him better than anybody else in the school. She can make the best recommendations for on-going programs. Test results are not as reliable as the opinion of a good teacher.

Mandated special education requirements have grown by leaps and bounds. These proliferating rules are a burden to the child study team because they make demands on its limited time. They are a burden to the school system because they make demands on its limited funds. If the state does not take action soon, special education is going to, as the expression goes, "kill the goose that laid the golden egg". Schools are going to balk at funding it.

Child study team members know that they have more to offer children than they are able to under the present mandates. It is time for the state department of education to consult them before more rules and regulations are added to an already overwhelmed child study team and all special education programs suffer.

17

Moral and Intellectual Autonomony

Once, at a school conference, I asked his teacher if my son was empathetic. "If he sees a classmate in difficulty, does he try to help?" "Does he express concern if a classmate is hurt?" "If another child needs help with his classwork, does he offer assistance?" She said she did not know because the children in her class were required to stay in their seats and were not permitted to talk. She emphasized the words "her class" and never referred to it as "our class".

Why do we continue to put children in a classroom together? The reason should be that children learn as much from each other as they do from the teacher—maybe more. They are intellectually stimulated by each other. They learn from the different ways of thinking of their classmates. They recognize and accept different learning styles.

Often, when a child makes a mistake, the teacher says "That's wrong." and asks another child for the "correct" answer. She can be much more helpful to the whole group if she says, "That's interesting. How did you arrive at that answer?"

The child's explanation usually will reveal some correctable misconception, but sometimes it may indicate that he is a divergent, creative thinker who sees things differently from the rest of the group. Understanding how such a student thinks would be interesting and helpful to everyone in the class. It also helps students to understand that there is more than one way to solve a problem.

Teachers, who insist that their students remain silent and immobile, tend to teach mainly by the lecture method. They stand in front of the class and do most of the talking. Usually, when they do interact, it is with one child at a time. Social Interaction and cooperative learning are discouraged. In classes run like this, little would be lost if the school system broke up the class and isolated each student in front of a TV monitor.

In such a system, the teacher gives lectures from a TV studio. The children interact with her, one at a time by pushing buttons and turning on query lights. The teacher then selects one of the lights and opens a channel for the question. The students do not interact with each other. This eliminates students talking and moving around which some teachers find threatening to their authority. This is not as far-fetched as it sounds; it is already being done where necessary to serve widely separated rural communities which have few children.

Teachers who keep tight control of their class and who do not permit, encourage and plan for interactions among the students not only waste valuable learning experiences, they retard the children's progress toward their full intellectual potential. It reminds me of a cartoon where the teacher says to the class: "This class will stimulate your ideas and thoughts . . . and remember, no talking." We all perceive how ridiculous this sounds and know instinctively that there will be little learning or creative thinking in that class.

A class is comprised of a group of people who work together for a common goal and are concerned about each other. The whole class, which includes the teacher, is involved and responsible not only for the successes of the group but for its failures. They all succeed and fail together. The students not only develop intellectually by learning together, they also grow morally by developing a concern for their peers. Children learn concern for others by observing and modeling adult behavior and by helping and working with each other.

Jean Piaget, the noted Swiss psychologist, stated that the aim of education is moral and intellectual autonomy. They go together. Everything we do in the name of education should have the potential for developing these two attributes in our children. Anything we do in the name of education which thwarts the development of these attributes should be re-evaluated and changed.

18

The Joy of Learning

There once was a great deal of press given to a comparison of the educational systems of our country and Japan. The results of a study entitled, "Japanese Education Today" praised the high level of overall academic achievement of the typical Japanese student. This level was achieved through a combination of high expectations, hard work, well-rewarded teachers and the heavy involvement of Japanese mothers in the education of their children.

The Japanese and perhaps the Chinese seemed to have no question about the purpose of education: it is to do well on standardized tests. In order to do well, knowledge needs to be conveyed by the teacher to the student. It is up to the student to remember what he has been taught so that he can answer the questions on the test. The ultimate goal is to be admitted to the most prestigious university. Once admitted, the students tend to relax and do not need to excel because they have already achieved their goal. The Japanese also admit that an emphasis on knowing the one right answer on the test, leads to conformity and lack of creativity.

The Japanese students are being taught that the purpose of education is to pass tests. The purpose of education in America ideally has been to make life-long learners of the students.

Hopefully, we would like to produce students who learn because there is an intrinsic value in simply finding an answer to a question. There should be some joy in the activity. In Japan, the joy seems to be in pleasing adults or in knowing you are the best test taker, or in knowing you can relax and enjoy yourself

Children will only become life-long learners if they take pleasure in the activity and they feel there is some useful purpose to it. Otherwise, they will stop as soon as they are left unsupervised. This is happening more and more. When children have a choice, they do not read a book, they watch television. We seem to forget that what we learn should be put to some use. We never seem to use our learning as a tool in order to take the next step or in order to find an answer. The child who does is our creative child. He learns because he wants to know and not because it is required. This attitude should be what we foster in all children.

A parent once came to me because she was anxious to know her son's reading level. I suggested she give him a book and listen to him read. She said he never opens a book. My comment was that showed her that he was a non-reader no matter what the test score indicates. Another parent complained that her child never reads at home and she felt it was the teacher's responsibility to make him read. I asked her if her son ever saw her husband or her reading. She said no because they did not have time and besides she did not enjoy reading.

While learning is hard work, children need to take some pleasure and joy in learning in order for it to have meaning and in order for what they learn to be put to use. Adults can be most helpful to children by modeling behavior which indicates that they learn because of the pleasure they get from learning and not because of the prestige involved or because someone else will notice and give them praise.

19

Science Literacy

A teacher informed a parent that her young son would be taken out of the regular class for short periods in order to receive extra help in reading. The parent expressed concern that her son would be missing something in the regular class. The school informed the parent that he would not miss things like recess, art or music. He would only miss science. Everybody, that includes parent, teacher, and child was satisfied with this arrangement. All agreed that the student, by missing the science program, would not miss anything important to his education.

Albert Shanker lamented the fact that our students, and that includes all of our outstanding students, perform less well on standardized tests as their counterparts in other countries. The students' scores were compared in math and science since they are the only ones that lend themselves to comparison among cultures. The conclusion seems to be that either our students, or our educational system or both are inferior to those in other countries.

Another and perhaps more reasonable explanation may be that many of our students receive no education in math and science at all. Other countries, in addition to having a longer school year, begin implementing an earnest science and math curriculum in the first grade. Math is taught together with science since math is the tool of science. We tend to teach subjects in isolation with no connection to the real, technological world the children are living in.

We are missing a golden opportunity by not learning from the success of other countries. Children are born scientists. They are naturally curious about every new thing they observe. Most are quickly discouraged from this curiosity and creativeness because nobody seems interested in their questions. By third grade, they do not ask: "Why is the sky blue?" "What makes grass green?" "Why does the light stop when I turn off the switch?" They just fill in the blanks in answer to adult's questions. Only a few cling to that precious inquisitiveness.

Nobel Prize winner, Leon Lederman, says: "Scientists are children who never grew up." Like Peter Pan they see magic in the way the natural world is put together. They delight in exploring. We may be denying our children this experience by the way we teach science or by not teaching math and science at all.

The problem may stem from the fact that many of our teachers are themselves victims of a poor science and math curriculum and feel uncomfortable teaching these subjects. That could be remedied by staff development programs for all elementary school teachers. Every teacher should know enough science so that she or he is equipped to answer children's questions or at least to be able to say, "Let's find out" and know how to do that.

The American Association for the Advancement of Science released the results of a four year study of science education in the public schools. In their study, "Benchmarks for Science Literacy" they recommend that children as young as five be given regular science lessons—not just scattered experiments like collecting snowflakes and learning that each snowflake has six points—but lessons given as often as reading. The study found that typical prevailing techniques require memorization, for example memorizing the 109 elements on the periodic table, rather than devising and testing theories or drawing conclusions from experimental data. The study makes no recommendations on national testing for fear that schools and teachers would take the recommended benchmarks for each grade and use them as test questions. Children should be learning science not just to pass tests, but to develop curiosity and understanding of the world around them.

The parent who did not object to having her son taken out of the science lesson in order to receive more help in reading probably was making the correct choice given the state of the present science curriculum in our schools. There will be no more American Nobel prize winners in science and perhaps no more American scientists unless we change our attitude towards science and math education.

20

Auditory Processing

If your child is failing in school and had ear problems as a baby, the difficulty may be due to poor auditory processing. This impairment seems to affect boys more than girls.

Some children cannot screen out conflicting noises and miss much of what is said. This problem often goes undetected because they can hear in a one-on-one situation when the adult looks right at them, but fail to get the message when competing sounds interfere. They cannot seem to ignore distractions.

A Central Auditory battery of standardized tests may be in order especially if you constantly describe your son as a child who never listens to anybody. Even without testing, however, you can begin to help your son if you suspect there is a problem.

Get his full attention before speaking to him. Stoop down to his level and make eye contact. When you are sure you have his full attention; make your sentences and requests short and concise. Then ask him to repeat back to you what you have just said to him. Do not talk to him when he has his back to you. He will not understand what you have said and you will both end up angry and frustrated.

You can help him to increase his ability to attend and to disregard distractions by means of games. One game might be to ask him to carry out a series of verbal commands in sequence. If he follows the sequence correctly, he wins the game and the prize. For example:" John there is something hidden in the third drawer of the bureau on the right side." "Find it and bring it to me." For other ideas for listening games, ask your librarian. Also, look for games for Christmas presents which involve listening and following directions.

Many elementary teachers make adjustments to their teaching style almost automatically when the child has difficulty processing information. They get the child's attention first and have him repeat the direction given. Middle school teachers, however, tend not to do this. In middle school, there are more teachers with more classes and more children to get to know.

These teachers tend to lecture while walking up and down the aisle. Children with processing problems miss most, if not all, of what is said. That is why this problem may not manifest itself until middle school.

Auditory processing problems do not necessarily mean a child has ear problems. The difficulty has to do with the brain not the ear. Any ear problems, once discovered, were probably corrected as a baby. In the meantime, however, the baby did not hear well when the "window of opportunity" for learning expressive and receptive language was open.

There are other children, however, who do have undiagnosed ear defects. Be concerned if your child is not disturbed by loud noises; does not respond when spoken to; uses gestures almost exclusively to establish needs rather than verbalizing; watches adults' faces intently; his attention wanders while someone is reading to him; often says "huh" or "what" indicating he does not understand; he breathes with his mouth open.

When hearing problems go undetected, children have problems in school which are usually attributed to other reasons. These children are restless, have short attention spans, are distracted in groups, and are seldom first to do what the teacher asks. In addition, they are unaware of social conventions like automatically saying, "thank you.", "I'm sorry". They grab another child to get his attention rather than saying his name and, in general, is unaware of disturbing others with noises.

Children with hearing problems may not be able to communicate or to use words as effectively as their peers. As a result they may appear to be less intelligent than they really are. When tested, they may do poorly because they do not understand the questions and may guess or say "I don't know." This appears to confirm the hypothesis of limited intelligence.

These children often have behavior problems because they are not sure what is expected of them.

Since most hearing problems are correctable, either through operations or hearing aids or education, it is important that parents be vigilant to catch them early.

21

Bullying

Most adults become incensed when they discover that there is bullying in their child's school. Immediately they advocate severe punishment of the bully. Now, who is the bully? As Pogo said, "We have met the enemy and he is us."

Severe punishments, policing and strict rules restricting their behavior will not cause bullies to relinquish their roles.

Such actions confirm them. These techniques merely put adults in the role of bullies. A much better approach, which also has the added advantage of modeling problem solving techniques, is for the adults to acknowledge that there is a problem and to work to develop programs aimed at solutions and prevention.

Schools are in the business of education. That means the education of all students including the bullies. One solution is to provide activities where students are given the opportunity to get to know each other and to learn how to interact in constructive ways.

One of the best ways to do this is through cooperative learning lessons. In the school setting, to complete assignments cooperatively, students must function as a "cooperative group". They must interact with each other, share ideas and materials, help each other learn, pool their information and resources, use division of labor when appropriate, integrate each member's contribution into a group product and facilitate each other's learning. As a result, communication, conflict management, and leadership skills are developed and in the process the students are given the opportunity to appreciate and to understand each other better.

Margaret Mead made the point that the future quality of human life, as well as the survival of the human species, will be dependent upon cooperative behavior along with a concern and respect for the rights of others. This behavior can be modeled, taught and nourished in the classroom.

Another solution involves providing opportunities for children to learn to empathize with each other. Bullies will only relinquish their dominance gained at the expense of others by the development of higher values such as empathy and consideration.

One way to do this is to help bullies feel what their victim feels. This can be done by the teacher listening to the victim in private and then conveying to a small group of his peers, which includes the bully, the distress of the victim. The teacher conveys to the group that they are not there to be blamed but for each member to offer to do something to help the victim feel better. This enables bullies to understand the extent of someone else's pain, which in severe cases, can lead to suicide. Some bullies are in so much pain themselves that they do not comprehend the pain they cause in others.

There are many other activities the school can institute to develop empathy in children. Students could be given the opportunity to help younger ones by reading to them. Older students could help others through leadership positions like being on a school council or being on the school patrol. Students could learn about those less fortunate than themselves through clothing drives, visits to nursing homes, or donating food to help the homeless. Teachers could stress empathy by such questions during the reading lesson as: "How do you think the person in the story feels?" "How would you feel if the same thing happened to you?" "What would you do to help that person?"

If there is bullying in your child's school, do not accept the school's position that it is normal and the school cannot do anything about it anyway. Something can and should be done not only for the victim's sake but for the bully's sake. Successful young bullies tend to grow up to become the hardened criminals who keep our jails full.

22

Encouragement

The most important thing you can do for children is to encourage them. Parents, teachers, and other adults who have children in their care need to understand an important principle of human behavior, i.e. children function best when they believe in themselves and know that other people believe in them also.

We need to believe in children and accept them as they are. The first step is to stop discouraging them by eliminating negative comments about them. We do not have to accept children's misbehavior but we should never say anything negative about them as people. We must learn to separate the deed from the doer.

Children should be helped to feel good about themselves. We do this by focusing on their strengths. This is never accomplished by telling them they can do better since that is a negative statement on what they have already done.

Some adults even manage to turn encouraging statements into discouraging ones: "It looks like you really worked hard on that . . . so why not do that all of the time?" Or "See what you can do when you really try?"

Encouragement is the prime motivator. Dr. Don Dinkmeyer, who has developed three programs based on Alfred Adler's philosophy, makes a useful distinction between praise and encouragement.

The basic difference between praise and encouragement is that praise is based on competition and is a value judgment while encouragement focuses on the effort and accepts children as they are.

Praise is for things well done. It is a reward and the child is valued by the adult. "You're a good boy." "You came in first. That's great." "I'm so proud of you."

Some children begin to rely on praise and only perform if they receive it. They may also begin to feel worthwhile only if they are on top which usually means at the expense of others. These children eventually may set unrealistic standards for themselves and learn to fear failure and refuse to take risks.

Words of encouragement, on the other hand, allow you to respond to a wide range of behavior. You focus on their strengths and assets. The words of encouragement are: "I have confidence in your judgment." "It looks as if you worked very hard on that." "I like the way you handled that." "How do you feel about that?"

Sometimes, when a child expresses discouragement, you might respond with: "Since you are not satisfied, what do you think you can do so that you will be pleased with it?" "You are making progress." "Looks like you are moving along." "You may not feel you have reached your goal, but look how far you have come."

Do not dwell on children's shortcomings, rather point out what they do right. Give help in the form of suggestions and be specific when possible. Encouragement does not compare one child with another and can be given when children feel bad about themselves and are down on themselves. We can focus on children's contributions and show we appreciate what they do for us.

Many of our children are discouraged, and discouraged children have difficulty learning. Adults who work with children need to have it within their power to counteract this. Children need and respond to encouragement. It takes practice to learn to be encouraging mainly because we have high standards for ourselves and the children in our care but, once learned it becomes automatic. I encourage you to try it, and I promise you will be astounded with the results.

I suggest you begin practicing by encouraging yourself, then you family. The next group that needs encouragement is teachers. Parents tend to communicate with the superintendent and School Board when they are dissatisfied, not when they are satisfied. This can be very discouraging to teachers. The next time you plan on giving a gift to a teacher or in some other way want to show your appreciation, write a letter to the teacher and send copies to the superintendent and the School Board. This is very is appropriate, very encouraging, and rarely done.

23

Does Your Child Really Have ADHD?

I just returned from John's graduation from high school. Not only did he graduate in 4 years, he received two blue ribbons for his sculptures, first honors as a senior and acceptance in to college to study graphic design. Pretty good for a kid who in first grade was diagnosed by the school system as having Attention Deficit Hyperactive Disorder (ADHD).

This is a cautionary tale for all parents who have a child so designated by the school system.

It is easier for the school system to put a label on a child and make it the child's problem, rather than the school examining its philosophy and possibly discovering that it is the school system's problem. By calling it the child's problem the system does not have to change to fit the child's educational needs. Instead the child must change to fit the system's needs.

You may say that the system does not know what the children's needs are. With all of the testing and evaluations done on children, the system does have the necessary data. The problem is nobody is in charge of interpreting them and making the necessary adjustments. It is somewhat like the dilemma facing the CIA and FBI. They had all the information and data needed to predict and to thwart terrorist strikes but nobody knew how or was assigned to correlate and to interpret the information. This is also true of special education programs. The law requires reams of testing but few people are trained and given the responsibility to correlate, to understand and to make practical use of all the data.

John's history, to which the school had access, indicated that he had frequent ear infections as a baby and subsequently had tubes in his ears.

He still was not talking at age three. When he did begin speaking, he mispronounced words and nobody understood him.

In first grade, John was placed in a small class of sixteen children because they all had communication problems. These children were taught using the reading program mandated for use by the whole school. It required that every student be taught by learning the sounds of the letters and then sounding out the words. This was something, since birth, John could not do. Consequently, although bright, he was not learning to read and he knew it.

The sixteen children in his class were not permitted to move from or in their seats. They were not permitted to talk. They were not even permitted to sound out the words while working in their workbooks because that too was regarded as talking.

The teacher taught the reading lesson to the whole class as a group strictly following the teacher's manual. She worked from the chalk board at the front of the room, away from the students. John was in a seat which not only made it difficult to hear the teacher but to see the chalkboard. He had to move in his seat in order to see the board.

Because John was not learning to read, the teacher referred him to the child study team. Before he was evaluated, the school counselor called his mother and told her that John was a DSM III-R attention-deficit, hyperactive-disorder (ADHD) child. She recommended to his mother that she take him to a neurologist because there could be a question of medication. Again, something was wrong with the child, not the program the child was in.

Testing indicated that John had high average intelligence, but had a problem with language. Since the system would not change its school-wide mandated reading program, John would have to change. The only other option the school could offer was for him to receive his reading instruction in the more flexible program in the learning disability class. Since this was not acceptable under the rules and regulations for the handicapped, the school was forced to create a Resource Room Program for students like John who required reading programs appropriate for their individual learning styles. John learned to read. Thus, his story had a happy ending.

You can have a happy ending for your child if you to learn to ask questions of the school system. Here is a partial list:

If the school system labels your child, ask for a description of the behavior that results in that label. One person's definition may not be another's. This is particularly true of the ADHD label which is often based on rating scales and checklists supplied by the teacher. Observation, not checklists, is the essential procedure necessary to describe this behavior.

Ask the question, "Why". Why does the child behave that way? For some children like John, he knows he's not doing well, but he does not know why or what to do about it. He might even begin to doubt his ability to do anything right. Or he might feel that he is not a good person because he is unable to do the school work, and he is letting his parents down. He might even be afraid of losing their love.

Remember these are children. They think and interpret their world and their place in it like children, not adults. They are concrete thinkers, not abstract. They need all the encouragement and support and understanding you can give them. Your role is to be their advocates and best friends.

There are a few children for whom medication might be indicated. Before you reach that conclusion, however, be sure you understand your child's role as a member of a very complex school system.

Finally, good teachers require school systems which encourage and nurture their talents.

About the Author

Dr. Nancy Devlin graduated from Hunter College with a degree in English and a Masters degree in Guidance and School Counseling. She taught elementary school in New York City, and in military-dependent schools in Germany, Denmark and Japan. She earned her Ph.D. in Educational Psychology at the University of California at Berkeley. She was a psychologist for twenty-two years in the Princeton Schools. She is a licensed psychologist, a family therapist and a nationally-certified school psychologist. She is married to a Physicist and they have three sons. She has published hundreds of newspaper articles on issues of education and child rearing. At present, she has a website and blog, www.Cassandrasclassroom. com providing information on education, parenting and related topics.

Printed in the United States
By Bookmasters